HOPE

For The

HEAVY HEART

COMFORT FOR THOSE WHO GRIEVE

Dr. Michael A. Cramer

Unless otherwise indicated, all Scripture quotations are taken from the New King James Version®. Copyright © 1982 by Thomas Nelson. Used by permission. All rights reserved.

Hope For The Heavy Heart / Dr. Michael A. Cramer. —1st ed.

Published for the Power For Living Ministry, Inc.

Produced by Franklin Publishing, Princeton, Texas.

Printed in the United States of America

Dedication

This book is lovingly dedicated to our beloved son, Joseph R. Cramer. The Lord called Joseph home on January 5, 2012, at the age of twenty-eight. We miss Joseph dearly and we think of him daily. Joseph is forever with the Lord, and always in our hearts. Our entire family looks forward to our reunion in heaven. In the meantime, we pray that God uses: "Hope For The Heavy Heart" to encourage every heavy heart, who reads this book.

God Bless You,
Mike and Cindi Cramer

————••••————

In Loving Memory of

JOSEPH R. CRAMER

May 15, 1983 – January 5, 2012

Beloved Son and Brother

Loving Husband and Daddy

————••••————

Special Thanks

I want to thank my beautiful wife, Cindi, for her loving and faithful support. She is the love of my life, my best friend, and my greatest encourager. Her quiet strength and gentle spirit enriches my life, and enhances our ministry. Writing this book was a difficult task, and I am very grateful for Cindi cheering me on to the finish line.

I also want to thank our children: Dr. Michael L. (Jaymie) Cramer; Major, USMC, Jacob (Julia) Cramer; and Hannah (Jake) Hueni. They have demonstrated courageous faith in the midst of the tremendous sorrow of losing their brother. Their lives are an inspiration to me.

Last, but certainly not least, I want to thank the Lord. There were many tender moments while writing this book, but the Lord manifested His strength in my weakness. Jesus said: "*With men these things are impossible, but with God all things are possible*" (Matthew 19:26). I am truly thankful that the Lord is faithful to His word.

Contents

Introduction

This author is no stranger to sorrow. As a father, I know the agonizing pain of losing a son. As a pastor, I have ministered to countless grieving families through the years. Rest assured, my experience with grief is not based on theory. It is up close and very personal.

The purpose of this book is to offer hope for the heavy heart. Each short chapter is designed to help those that are deeply hurting. The bite-sized amounts of spiritual nutrition are included to strengthen the inner spirit. My goal is to comfort the walking wounded, who often suffer in silence.

Nobody escapes the heartbreak of losing a loved one. The grave is constantly calling people from all walks of life. Grief simply plays no favorites. At some point in time, everybody loses somebody.

Walking through the valley of the shadow of death is very painful. There is not any magic formula to soothe a hurting soul. Every person grieves in their own way. The search for comfort is universal, but the source of comfort is deeply personal.

My friend, I am truly very sorry for your loss. I wish I could wave a magic wand and erase your pain. Unfortunately, grief is a sad reality of life. My prayer is that God will use this book to encourage you with: Hope for your Heavy Heart.

1
Uncharted Waters

The sudden and unexpected loss of our twenty-eight year old son was devastating. There had been no time to prepare and no chance to say good-bye. Without any advance notice, our journey on the ship of life had just set sail for uncharted waters.

Losing a loved one is like having your heart ripped out of your chest. The pain from the crushing blow causes your heart to feel shattered beyond repair. Time seems to stand still, as the sorrow sinks deep into your soul. The relentless pain in your heart is almost impossible for your mind to process.

Finding the strength to carry on, while carrying the burden of a broken heart, is possibly the biggest challenge in life. There is not any magic wand to wave the grief away. There is not any special formula to soften the sorrow. Setting sail on the high seas of sorrow does not come with a compass to guide your trip. Everyone must travel their own uncharted waters in the soul-searching quest for peace in the midst of the storm.

There are many painful moments on the tumultuous trip of uncharted waters. Initially, there are gut-wrenching decisions such as: selecting a proper casket, choosing a special cemetery plot, writing a descriptive obituary, choosing beautiful flowers, gathering personal pictures for public display, selecting music for a video presentation, and planning an honorable funeral service, just to name a few. Unfortunately, the painful journey has just begun. Navigating the uncharted waters of grief in search of comfort is a life-long process.

Fortunately, there is hope for the heavy heart. The Word of God says: *"The Lord is near to those who have a broken heart"* (Psalm 34:18). The Lord is always just a simple prayer away. Talk to God and pour out your broken heart to Him. The Lord cares for you and He will comfort your heart with His love.

You can also draw strength from the Lord, as you read and reflect upon His Word. You will feel the comforting presence of the Spirit of God, as you drink deeply from the well of the Word of God. In the precious passage of Scripture, the Twenty-Third Psalm, the Lord offers to be our shepherd, as we walk through the valley of the shadow of death.

My friend, don't lose hope and don't lose heart. You do not have to walk the road alone. The Lord promises to be near you and He will walk with you every step of the way. Let the Lord be your shepherd, and He will be your faithful guide through the uncharted waters of grief. Lean on the Lord, and He will give: Hope for your heavy heart.

2
After the Casseroles

Word spreads like wildfire when the hand of death knocks on the door of your life. Family and friends appear out of nowhere, and stop by your house to offer their condolences. Many generously bring casseroles that can be served at your convenience. It is a gracious gesture that also serves as a symbol of comfort. The flood of visitors continues until you have enough food to feed an army.

In a few days, people attend the visitation and their presence brings you comfort. Their expression of love is like a ray of sunshine on a cloudy day. You welcome their hugs and are thankful for their support in your time of need. The outpouring of love continues during the funeral service, as you try to wrap your mind around your broken heart.

After the funeral, family and friends join the caravan to the cemetery. It is comforting to know that others are going with you on the saddest drive of your life. The moment you have been dreading is rapidly approaching. The time has come to say your final good-bye at the grave. You pray for your loved one to rest in peace, and leave a piece of your heart in the process.

Then you travel to the church, or community center, for a meal prepared with loving hands and compassionate hearts. Your family and friends remain by your side, as you fellowship and break bread together. The delicious casseroles nourish your weary body, and the soothing atmosphere comforts your wounded soul.

However, after the casseroles are gone, the lonely reality of grief begins. The tidal wave of initial support, soon becomes a trickle of occasional encouragement. Eventually, your phone stops ringing, the text messages and emails stop appearing, and the sympathy cards stop arriving. The empty casserole pans become a symbol of the empty feeling in the pit of your stomach.

Try not to be too hard on your friends. They still care about you, but probably do not comprehend the depth of your sorrow. Their confusion of your grief should not be interpreted as a lack of concern for your emotional pain. Most likely, you are still in their thoughts and prayers, even though they may not mention it.

Fortunately, the Lord has not abandoned you. God says: *"Fear not, for I am with you; Be not dismayed, for I am your God. I will strengthen you, Yes, I will help you, I will uphold you with My righteous right hand"* (Isaiah 41:10). The Lord also promises to: *"never leave you nor forsake you"* (Hebrews 13:5).

My friend, after the casseroles are gone, rest assured, God is still present. Christ cares deeply about your grief, and He loves you with great compassion. Listen carefully to His Word, and the Holy Spirit will gently whisper: Hope for your heavy heart.

3
Wait for the Fog to Lift

Grief can settle over your soul like a dense fog. It is very difficult to navigate your life when intense sorrow is blinding your eyes. The loss of a loved one can blur your vison with tears, and block your view of tomorrow. It is absolutely essential to wait for the fog to lift.

The fog of grief does not lift overnight. It takes time to see your way clear. That is one reason that it is wise to hold off on major decisions. Give yourself some time to regain your bearings when life has knocked you off balance.

Jesus emphasized the phrase "*a little while*" when comforting His disciples (John 16:16-19). Our Lord informed them that sorrow was on the horizon, but comfort was also on the way. This confused the disciples, and they asked for some clarification. In essence, Jesus advised them to wait *a little while* for the fog to lift. Then they would see the hand of God at work.

Waiting for the fog to lift is good advice for anyone experiencing grief. Following your heart when it is burdened with sorrow may lead you in the wrong direction. A good rule of thumb is to consider waiting a year before making any life changing decisions.

When fog settles over a community, the schools often have a two hour delay. The fog does not cancel the entire day, it simply postpones the start of the day. This reduces the danger of travel and protects the safety of the students. Once the fog lifts, safe travel resumes, and the school day proceeds as planned.

In a similar way, Jesus advises us to wait *a little while,* and proceed with caution. It is very wise to be careful, as you travel through the dense fog of heart-breaking sorrow. In time, when you are thinking more clearly, you will be more capable of proceeding with confidence.

My friend, give yourself some time to allow the fog of grief to lift from your life. In *a little while,* you will be better prepared to make decisions about the future. In the meantime, focus on your faith, and watch God give: Hope for your heavy heart.

4
Carry on with Courage

I prefer the term "carry on" instead of "move on." The loss of a loved one is something you carry with you for the rest of your life. You don't move on from the cherished memories and the special place your loved one held in your heart. The loss of life will never eliminate your bond of love. We carry on with courage and trust the Lord to give hope to our heavy heart.

Sometimes, well-meaning people may suggest that it is time to move on with life. As if there is some magic wand to wave and make everything wonderful again. That is hollow advice from shallow people. Ignore it. One of the realities of death is that it causes us to go below the surface of life. Shallow people will never understand your deep pain.

Fortunately, the Lord promises to give you the strength to carry on with courage. The Scripture says: *"Be of good courage, and He shall strengthen your heart, all you who hope in the Lord"* (Psalm 31:24). The Lord will help you put one foot in front of the other, as you face the future, without forgetting the past.

It takes tremendous courage to carry on when everything within you wants to throw in the towel.

When you feel like you are drowning in despair, the Lord offers a life jacket of hope. He will gently whisper in your ear words of hope for your heavy heart. He will walk with you and carry your burden, as you carry on with courage.

The motivation to carry on is nothing short of a miracle. The supernatural strength from the Lord is an encouraging experience. The peace of mind that comes from the presence of the Holy Spirit will comfort your soul. Lean on the Lord and lean into His love. Take life one step at a time, and when it seems like you can't carry on another step, let the Lord carry you.

Rest assured, the Lord has not forgotten you. He cares very deeply for you and offers to strengthen your heart. Trust Him to give you the courage to carry on. The Lord wants to wrap the brokenness of your life with the blanket of His love.

My friend, there is hope in the midst of despair when your faith is focused on the Lord. Don't lose hope, and carry on with the love of our Lord. With the help of our comforting Savior, you can carry on like a courageous soldier. Keep the faith, and God will give: Hope for your heavy heart.

5
Blind-Sided

The loss of a loved one can leave you feeling emotionally blind-sided. Especially when the death was unexpected. When there was no way to see it coming, it was nearly impossible to prepare for. It may have caught you totally off guard and knocked you completely off your feet. Getting knocked off balance is unsettling, but getting knocked out of the ring is devastating.

The knock-out punch that comes out of nowhere is a stunning blow. You find yourself face down on the ground, wondering how you even landed there. You hardly have the strength to lift your head to take a look around. The idea of grabbing the ropes and pulling yourself back up to your feet is hard to imagine. The thought of climbing back into the ring does not even cross your mind. Bouncing back from being blind-sided is an extremely difficult challenge.

After we lost our son, I said the following words: "I don't know if I can bounce back from this one." It was not that my faith doubted the Lord. My life had been rocked to the core, but my faith was still anchored to the Rock. However, for the first time in my life, I found myself wondering if I had the strength to bounce back from being so blind-sided.

The reality was that I did not have the strength within me, but there was strength from the Lord above me.

The Scripture says: *"God is our refuge and strength, a very present help in trouble"* (Psalm 46:1). The word "refuge" is a beautiful term. God provides a place of safety and shelter to protect us during the storms of life. He strengthens our soul with the peace of His presence. God whispers in our ear and tells us that He loves us, He is with us, and He cares deeply for us. God is always available to help us at any time, and He offers His special help during the difficult times. We can take refuge in God, and trust in His protective care.

The burden of being blind-sided by grief is so great that sometimes we don't even know what to pray. In those moments, it can be helpful to simply wait before the Lord in a humble spirit of prayer. According to Romans 8:26, the Holy Spirit steps in during our unbearable pain, and prays for us in a deeply personal and powerful way. This supernatural encounter with God is difficult to explain, but very comforting to experience.

My friend, when sorrow has knocked you down, the Savior will not let you get knocked out. The Lord will pick you up, dust you off, and gently put you on your feet again. God will comfort your wounded soul, and strengthen your inner spirit with the power of His Holy Spirit. When the burden of grief has blind-sided your life, the Lord will lovingly carry your burden, faithfully sustain you with His grace and give: Hope for your heavy heart.

6
Pain Management

The loss of a loved one leaves an enormous hole in your heart, which causes tremendous emotional pain. Initially, the pain is so intense, it is hard to imagine how to cope with it. Hang in there. In time, you will learn to manage the pain better, even though it will never be totally eliminated.

When we lost our son, an emotional dam broke, and a river of tears flooded my soul. The pain that gripped my heart would not let go. It was very difficult to concentrate on anything because the grief captivated everything. I simply had to hold on to the hope that, eventually, I would learn to manage the pain in my heart.

I found hope for my heavy heart by heeding the words of King David, when he said: *"I would have lost heart, unless I had believed that I would see the goodness of the Lord in the land of the living. Wait on the Lord; be of good courage, and He shall strengthen your heart; Wait, I say on the Lord!"* (Psalm 27:13-14).

Sometimes, in the midst of deep sorrow, we simply have to trust that the Lord will give us the strength to survive. It is like holding on to a log while being swept down a raging river. To keep from losing your grip, and getting swept away by the current, you have to believe that smooth waters will eventually surface. The thought that the Lord will not make us wait until heaven to experience His goodness, inspires us with hope on the horizon.

One vital key to pain management is to simply wait on the Lord. This takes courageous faith because God does not give us a time frame for waiting on Him. God blesses our total trust in His promise to strengthen our heart. God provides His peace to calm the storm in our soul.

Just like a wounded animal learns to patiently wait on Mother Nature, we must learn to patiently wait on Father God. When an animal is wounded it will lay down and remain perfectly still. Over the process of time, an amazing thing often happens. Mother Nature goes to work, and provides an inner strength to manage the pain, and miraculously heal the wound.

My friend, in a much greater way, Father God is able to strengthen you. He can comfort your inner pain with His inspirational presence. Time will not totally heal the wound, but in time you will learn to manage the pain. Wait on the Lord and trust in His Word. The hope of seeing your loved one again in heaven, will inspire your life on earth with: Hope for your heavy heart.

7
Channel of Comfort

A reservoir is a large container to hold water. A river is a large channel to carry water. In our grief, we can either become a reservoir of comfort, or a channel of comfort. If we function like a reservoir, our focus will be upon receiving comfort from others. If we function like a river, our focus will be on giving comfort to others. God can use our pain as a platform of credibility to connect with others in pain.

The Scripture says: *"Blessed be the God and Father of our Lord Jesus Christ, the Father of mercies and God of all comfort, who comforts us in all our tribulation, that we may be able to comfort those who are in any trouble, with the comfort with which we ourselves are comforted by God"* (II Corinthians 1:3-4). In other words, God comforts us in order for us to be a channel of His comfort to others.

Shortly after we lost our son, my wife and I went to Florida for a couple of weeks. We really did not feel like going, but we had already purchased the airline tickets, rented a car, and reserved our lodging. We literally had to use it or lose it. With great reluctance, we decided to go on vacation.

Since we serve in ministry and are in the public spotlight, it was helpful to be able to grieve in private. We walked the beach, watched the sunset, and held on to one another. We poured out our broken hearts to the Lord, and sought comfort from His Word.

One day, my wife and I decided to travel an hour to visit a recent widow that we knew. She had lost her husband a few months before, and our church hosted the funeral. Our surprise visit was welcomed with open arms. You would have thought we showed up with a million dollars. She was delighted to see us. We comforted one another with encouraging words, a listening ear, and a shoulder to lean on.

It was a tremendous blessing to serve as a channel of comfort. We saw a glimpse of the purpose of our pain. It gave us a greater sensitivity to someone else in sorrow. We were better able to empathize with her pain, and God used us as a channel of His comfort. My wife and I both commented that it was the best day of our vacation that particular year.

My friend, many times, God has used our loss to connect with others in need of comfort. It does not eliminate our pain, but it provides a sense of purpose. God can do the same through your grief. Let God's mercy flow through you like a river, and become a channel of His comfort to others. In this process, the Lord will also bless you with: Hope for your heavy heart.

8
The Empty Chair

When it comes to seating arrangements, many people are creatures of habit. Religious people often sit in the same seat at their regular place of worship. Sports fans can usually be found sitting in the same seat, or at least the same section, at sporting events. Family members often sit in the same seat at the table during family meals. To borrow a quote from the late Walter Cronkite, as he would complete his evening news broadcast: "And that's the way it is."

The empty chair is one of the things that makes family gatherings so delicate after the loss of a loved one. It is a visual reminder of the one that is no longer with us. At first, the chair may literally be left empty. Family members may find it difficult to sit in the seat where their loved one used to sit. Even if the chair is occupied at the table, there is still the visual metaphor of the empty chair. It is symbolic of the loved one that has passed away.

The empty chair reminds us of the empty feeling we have in our hearts. A family member is missing and it hurts. Special gatherings such as: Thanksgiving, Christmas, Easter, Birthdays, and other family events take on a new dimension. Death changes the dynamics of family life.

Try and fill the empty chair with fond memories of the loved one that used to sit there. Tell endearing stories of positive character qualities, which made that family member so special. Take turns sharing ways they touched your life, and the influence they had on the family. Death may rob us of personal moments with our loved one, but it cannot rob our precious memories. It has been said that the memory is a gift from God that not even death can destroy.

The Apostle Paul said: "*I thank my God upon every remembrance of you*" (Philippians 1:3). It is a healthy practice to thank the Lord for the way He uses people to touch our lives. It does not have to be Thanksgiving Day to thank the Lord for the many fond memories of our loved one.

By the way, it is also healthy to show gratitude for those that are still with us. Take turns at the dinner table, and express your love and appreciation for each family member present. It can transform the atmosphere of the room. The positive experience blesses the family, and lifts some of the burden off their heavy hearts.

The Scripture says: "*Pleasant words are like a honeycomb, sweetness to the soul, and health to the bones*" (Proverbs 16:24). My friend, sharing fond memories of our loved one, and speaking kind words to one another, is a sweet and healthy experience. It may not replace the empty chair, but it is part of the healing process that provides: Hope for your heavy heart.

9
Fork in the Road

The loss of a loved one is a fork in the road in your journey of faith. The intense pain will either draw you closer to the Lord, or drive you further away from the Lord. Facing grief will definitely become a defining moment in your life.

Initially, the sorrow can feel almost suffocating. Don't let the pain push you toward the wrong path. The relentless anguish may create a desire to seek emotional relief though various forms of self-medication. This desire is not about seeking pleasure; it is about escaping pain. In this fork in the road of your life, allow the grief to guide you toward the Lord.

The Psalmist prayed: *"Hear my cry, O God; Listen to my prayer. From the end of the earth I will cry to you. When my heart is overwhelmed; lead me to the Rock that is higher than I"* (Psalm 61:1-2). My friend, this rock is the Lord Jesus Christ. He is the rock that will not roll.

When you are travelling the path of heartbreak and shattered dreams, you will come to a fork in the road. In that moment of truth, turn to the Lord. You will discover genuine comfort for your grieving soul. Pour out your heart to God in prayer. God listens because He cares for you. God will comfort your heart with His peace, which surpasses all human understanding.

Turning away from the Lord is a dead end street. It will take you down a path of anger, bitterness, and self-destruction. You don't want to take that path. It will only add to your sorrow and increase your pain. There is a better direction that leads to hope for your heavy heart.

Turning to the Lord will not erase the pain, but it will ease the pain. God will help you manage the pain, as He soothes your soul with the presence of His Spirit. The Word of God will anchor your life to the rock-solid foundation of faith in Christ. The Lord will meet your deepest needs through the power of prayer, and the strength of His Word.

My friend, when you come to this fork in the road, take the path that will draw you closer to the Lord. He is patiently waiting to walk with you, one step at a time. Reach out your hand to the Lord, and He will take you by the hand to give: Hope for your heavy heart.

10
Hope for the Heavy Heart

Our reunion in heaven is the ultimate hope for every heavy heart on earth. Jesus comforted His disciples with the promise of heaven, and the same promise holds true today. The fact that we will see our loved ones again, inspires our faith in the future.

Jesus said: *"Let not your heart be troubled; you believe in God, believe also in Me"* (John 14:1). The word "troubled" is the idea of being worried to the point of despair. It is a word picture that describes a piece of cloth that is unravelling, and coming apart at the seams. Jesus is literally saying that faith in Him will keep your life from falling apart.

The disciples had heavy hearts because they were about to be separated from the Lord. Jesus was going away, and it was unclear when they would see Him again. Therefore, the Lord set their minds at ease, and calmed their fears with the promise of a future reunion.

There is hope for the heavy heart when we remain confident in Christ. Believing in Christ is simply taking Him at His Word. Jesus is who He claimed to be, and He accomplished what He was sent to do.

There is hope for the heavy heart when we receive comfort from Christ. Jesus is preparing a real place called heaven, and He promises to take believers there. It will be a glorious reunion with the Lord, and with our loved ones that are waiting for us in heaven.

Jesus said: *"In My Father's house are many mansions; if it were not so, I would have told you. I go to prepare a place for you. And if I go and prepare a place for you, I will come again and receive you to Myself; that where I am, there you may be also"* (John 14:2-3). It is very comforting to know that our loved ones are with the Lord, and we will see them again.

Heaven is a beautiful place with walls of jasper and streets pure as gold. The river of life flows down from the throne of God. There is no sickness, no sorrow, no pain, no suffering, no tears of grief, and no sad good-byes. The thought of our future communion with the Lord, and reunion with our loved ones, makes me homesick for heaven.

Ultimately, there is hope for the heavy heart when we respond to the call of Christ. Jesus said: *"I am the way, the truth, and the life. No one comes to the Father except through Me"* (John 14:6). The entrance to heaven is through the doorway of Christ. The good news is that God loves you, and Christ is holding the door of heaven open to welcome you.

My friend, faith is trusting in the person and work of Christ. Jesus is the God-Man, who died and rose again for the sins of the entire human race. The resurrection of Jesus Christ proves that you can trust His Word. Affirm your faith in Christ, and accept His gift of eternal life. Believe in His promise of heaven, and you will receive: Hope for your heavy heart.

11
A Club Nobody Wants to Join

The loss of a child places a parent in a club nobody wants to join. You do not choose this club on your own. This club chooses you. Anybody that belongs to this group, knows the deep sorrow of a shattered dream.

Losing a child is like having your heart ripped out of your chest. There is no way to be prepared for this type of pain. It is undoubtedly the most heart-breaking experience that any parent could ever face. Anyone that has experienced the tragic loss of a child, would not wish the pain on their worst enemy.

My wife and I know the crushing pain of losing a child. Your knees buckle under the weight of the overwhelming sorrow. Your circle of life is knocked off balance, as the natural order of life spins out of control. Children expect to bury their parents, but parents do not expect to bury their children.

There is a mystery of a life cut short. No one can fully understand the reason that God allows such tragedies. The Scripture says: "*The secret things belong to the Lord our God...*" (Deuteronomy 29:29).

Some things we have to leave with the Lord. Some answers will simply have to wait until heaven.

The Scripture says: *"For we walk by faith, not by sight"* (II Corinthians 5:7). Faith is total trust in God. We do not need complete understanding, to have a confident trust in God.

When King David struggled for answers, he pictured himself like a trusting child, resting in the lap of God. He humbly stated: *"Surely I have calmed and quieted my soul, like a weaned child with his mother; like a weaned child is my soul within me"* (Psalm 131:2). His trust in God also encouraged others to: *"Hope in the Lord from this time forth and forever"* (Psalm 131:3).

When David lost an infant son, he said: *"I shall go to him, but he shall not return to me"* (II Samuel 12:23). The powerful king was not exempt from membership in a lonely club of broken hearts. But the promise of a future reunion in heaven, inspired his heart with hope.

My friend, faith is the only way to survive a club nobody wants to join. When sorrow sinks deep into your soul, crawl into the lap of our Heavenly Father. Grief may blur our vision with tears, but it does not have to blind our eyes from humble trust. Lean into the love of God, and trust Him to give: Hope for your heavy heart.

12
Lord, Pass Along Our Love

Several years ago, I visited a friend who had tragically lost two of his three teenage children in an automobile accident. There had been no time to say good-bye. By the time he and his wife arrived at the hospital, their beloved children had already gone to heaven. The sadness in his misty eyes told the story of the sorrow in his heavy heart.

During our conversation, he shared with me that sometimes in prayer, he asks the Lord to pass along his love to his children in heaven. It was a beautiful expression of his faith in the Lord, hope of heaven, and love for his children. It was a very moving conversation that left a deep impression on my life.

I had no idea the Lord was preparing me for a similar prayer, ten years down the road. After we lost our son, our prayers at family gatherings took on a new dimension. Now when we say grace before the meal at family functions, we ask the Lord to pass along our love to Joseph. It provides a spiritual connection with our son in heaven, and a sacred reflection of his place in our home.

The Scripture says: "*We are confident, yes, well pleased rather to be absent from the body and to be present with the Lord*" (II Corinthians 5:8). In other words, when a believer passes away, their soul leaves their body and immediately goes to be with the Lord. Yes, their soul is instantaneously ushered to their new home in heaven.

My friend, let's connect the dots. If our loved one is with the Lord, and we are talking to the Lord, it makes total sense to ask the Lord to pass along our love. You are literally talking to the Lord, who is at the same location as your loved one. I believe our Lord is happy to pass along our love in heaven. This aspect of prayer will inspire you with: Hope for your heavy heart.

13
Walking Through the Valley

Walking through the valley of grief is a very difficult journey. On one side is a mountain of despair, and on the other side is a mountain of discouragement. In between, we face a deep valley, which is overshadowed with the pain of losing a loved one. Desperately, we ask the Lord, our Shepherd, to lead us to the green pastures of hope for our heavy heart.

Walking through the valley of heartbreak is like a nightmare. We wish we could wake up one day, and discover that it was just a bad dream. However, each morning reminds us of the sad reality of the loss of our loved one. Therefore, we roll out of bed, put one foot in front of the other, and search for the still waters to restore our soul.

The walking wounded keep marching through the valley, fully aware that their wound will never totally heal. A scab eventually develops over our heavy heart, but specific days will pick the scab. This causes the pain in our soul to rush to the surface. This cycle of sorrow is ignited by birthdays, holidays, anniversaries, and the annual reminder of our loved one's passing.

The "Happy Holidays" cry out for hope for the heavy heart. A Thanksgiving feast is hard to swallow with a lump in our throat. Christmas is less merry than before, due to the empty chair at the gift exchange. Ringing in the New Year with a big party is less appealing. It is just not easy to have a joyful celebration, as we soldier on with sadness tugging at our heart.

Walking through the valley of sorrow is a lonely experience, but we don't have to travel the road alone. The Psalmist said: *"Yea, though I walk through the valley of the shadow of death, I will fear no evil; For You are with me; Your rod and Your staff, they comfort me"* (Psalm 23:4). Rest assured, the Lord is ready, willing, and able to walk with us every step of the way.

My friend, The Good Shepherd wants to gently guide you through the dark valley of losing a loved one. Trust in the Lord, and you will sense the peace of His presence. Pour out your heart to God in prayer, and He will comfort your life with: Hope for your heavy heart.

14
The Fatigue of Grief

The emotional drain of losing a loved one is exhausting. I have always been a high energy person, but after we lost our son, I was tired all the time. I literally had no idea about the fatigue of grief.

I was tired during the day, yet, it was difficult to sleep at night. It was a strange cycle of sleepless nights and exhausting days. The night passed slowly, and the morning came much too soon.

The energy drained from my body like a run-down battery. The physical exhaustion left me feeling emotionally fragile. The lack of sleep amplified the pain in my heart, and the lump in my throat.

The fatigue of grief had placed me on the learning curve of life. My dependence on the Lord took on a whole new meaning. The promises in the Word of God brought hope to my heavy heart. The Lord sustained me with His grace and strengthened me with His Spirit.

The Scripture says: *"But those who wait on the Lord shall renew their strength; they shall mount up with wings like eagles, they shall run and not be weary, they shall walk and not faint"* (Isaiah 40:31). The Lord used His promise to give me the power to persevere. Eventually, the Lord energized my life by restoring my strength, and revitalizing my soul.

I have a plaque on the wall of my office containing that verse and a picture of an eagle. My wife gave it to me many years ago for Christmas. It has always been special, but after we lost our son, it became an even more treasured gift. Every day when I walk into my office, I am reminded of the faithfulness of God that overcomes the fatigue of grief.

My friend, believing the promise of God will help you put one foot in front of the other. It will give you the strength to take one day at a time. Wait patiently on the Lord, and trust in the power of His Word. God will strengthen your life and give: Hope for your heavy heart.

15
The Great Burden Bearer

Our Lord is described several ways in the New Testament. Jesus is our Savior. At the birth of Christ, the angel announced: *"For there is born to you this day in the city of David a Savior, who is Christ the Lord"* (Luke 2:11).

Christ is our Lord. The Apostle Paul declared: *"that at the name of Jesus every knee should bow... and every tongue should confess that Jesus Christ is Lord to the glory of God the Father"* (Philippians 2:10-11).

Jesus is our Shepherd. He is the *Good Shepherd* that gave His life for His sheep (John 10:11); the *Great Shepherd* that watches over His sheep (Hebrews 13:20); and the *Chief Shepherd* that will return for His sheep (I Peter 5:4).

The Lord is our friend. Jesus said: *"Greater love has no one than this, than to lay down one's life for his friends. You are my friends if you do whatever I command you"* (John 15:13-14). He is also described as: *"A friend that sticks closer than a brother"* (Proverbs 18:24).

All of those titles are special, but during our overwhelming sorrow, Jesus offers to be: The Great Burden Bearer. Christ carries us when the burden seems unbearable. When you feel like you are going to collapse under the weight of grief, Jesus steps in and carries your burden.

Jesus said: *"Come to Me, all you who labor and are heavy laden, and I will give you rest. Take My yoke upon you and learn from Me, for I am gentle and lowly in heart, and you will find rest for your souls. For My yoke is easy and My burden is light"* (Matthew 11:28-30). In this great invitation, Jesus welcomes us to team up with Him, and He will carry the burden.

Jesus carries our burden with memories that are unforgettable. Sharing fond memories with family and friends will keep your loved one alive in your mind. Cherish the pictures, video clips, and slide presentations, which bring your loved one to life in your heart.

Jesus also carries our burden with His love that is unconditional. Jesus said: *"For God so loved the world that He gave His only begotten Son, that whoever believes in Him should not perish but have everlasting life"* (John 3:16). This precious promise of the unconditional love of God is the heart and soul of the New Testament.

My friend, let Jesus be your Great Burden Bearer. The Lord will carry your unbearable burden of grief with His unconditional love. Jesus will comfort you with His tender compassion. Team up with Christ and He will provide: Hope for your heavy heart.

16
Sweet Dreams

Dreams can be a sweet source of Divine comfort. A mysterious form of communication can sometimes take place during our sleep. The longing of our heart may open up the mind to receive a message of hope. Nature may use our subconscious mind to nurture our grieving soul.

Shortly after we lost our son, I had a very vivid dream about him. We were sitting at the kitchen table and talking together. As Joseph and I conversed with one another, we both knew that it could not last. Eventually, he stood up to leave, and I knew it was time for him to go. We hugged and spoke of our love for each other.

Then in my dream, I said to Joseph: "Oh how I wish you could stay." He responded, "Now Dad, you know that I can't stay. I just wanted to stop by and tell you that I love you." We hugged again, and I walked him to the front door. Then Joseph opened the door and vanished out of sight. It was an incredible dream.

I awakened immediately after the dream was over. It was so real that I thanked the Lord for the dream. It was as if the Lord gave me a supernatural moment with my son. I did not sleep another wink that night, as I sat in wonder at the experience.

Several weeks later, I actually asked the Lord for another dream. In His gracious mercy, God answered my prayer. A couple nights later, I dreamed that Joseph and I were walking along the beach. We talked together and verbally expressed our love for each other. Then I said: "I know that you can't stay, so let's just enjoy this moment we have together." He smiled and nodded in approval. Then as we were walking together, he vanished into the heavens. As I woke up from my sleep, I thanked the Lord for touching my broken heart with a beautiful dream.

Through the years, the Lord has given me several sweet dreams about Joseph. They vary from fond memories of his childhood, to special family moments during his adult life. The dreams always include a bonding moment of a loving hug, and our verbal communication of love. The dreams always refresh my soul with a special dose of hope for my heavy heart.

The Scripture says: *"Weeping may endure for a night, but joy comes in the morning"* (Psalm 30:5). That passage of Scripture concludes by saying: *"You have turned for me my mourning into dancing; you have put off my sackcloth and clothed me with gladness. To the end that my glory may sing praise to You and not be silent, O Lord my God, I will give thanks to You forever"* (Psalm 30:11-12).

My friend, God can bring joy in the morning by providing a sweet dream at night. He may bless you with a special dream, or simply provide a vivid recollection of a fond memory. This loving touch from the hand of God will put a song in your heart, a spring in your step, and praise on your lips. Yes, sweet dreams can be a Divine Dose of: Hope for your heavy heart.

17
Facing Painful Flashbacks

The anxiety of facing painful flashbacks is hard to explain, but easy to understand, for anyone that has gone through the experience. The death of a loved one produces painful memories that linger in the back of your mind. Certain events can trigger a vivid scene that causes you to relive the deep-rooted sadness. It is like stepping into a time machine, which immediately transports your mind back to the initial moment of heartbreak.

For example, it can be very difficult to go back to the church, or funeral home, where the Memorial Service was held. When you walk into the room, you may experience a flashback of the unbearable scene of your loved one in the casket. The very place where people once gathered to comfort you, may now cause discomfort for your heavy heart.

There are several things that trigger my own painful flashbacks. Seeing a casket being loaded into a hearse, resurrects the tremendous pain of seeing our son being placed into the back of the hearse. A slide presentation, at any event, can bring to my mind the video presentation at the funeral of our son. The sorrow automatically surfaces from the deep recesses of my soul.

Facing painful flashbacks is an ongoing struggle. Places that once brought happiness, may produce a sense of sadness. Favorite vacation locations, which we once enjoyed as a family, are difficult to visit today. The same is true with attending certain sporting events. Even church activities can be challenging at times. Because I see so many clear reminders of Joseph, it is still very hard to believe that he is actually gone. I am confident that you feel the same way about your loved one.

Facing painful flashbacks requires prayer, and mountain moving faith. Jesus said: *"Have faith in God. For assuredly, I say to you, whoever says to this mountain, 'Be removed and cast into the sea,' and does not doubt in his heart, but believes that those things he says will come to pass, he will have whatever he says. Therefore I say to you, whatever things you ask when you pray, believe that you receive them, and you will have them"* (Mark 11:22-24).

Jesus is equating mountains to enormous challenges in life. Few things are more difficult to face than painful flashbacks. The good news is that we have access to the power of God through prayer. God honors our mountain moving faith by blessing our life with His strength.

My friend, God will help you face your painful flashbacks. Jesus will comfort your heart with peace, and conquer your challenging mountain of pain. Focus on His power, and claim His promises by faith. Allow the love of God to transform your painful flashbacks into a beautiful portrait of His grace. Trust in Christ, and He will give: Hope for your heavy heart.

18
Grief Relapse

Grief can be like the waves of an ocean. Just as the waves keep splashing on the shore, pain keeps pounding on your heavy heart. This cycle of sorrow can seem relentless. About the time you feel like you are gaining a grip on life, a sense of sadness may sweep over you like a tidal wave.

Don't be too hard on yourself when you experience a grief relapse. It is unrealistic to think we can eliminate all unexpected feelings of sorrow. Without any warning, certain memory triggers of tender moments can flood your mind. This may cause a brief setback on the road to emotional recovery. That is okay. Remember, three steps forward, and two steps backward, is still progress.

It is almost like a scab forms to protect your wounded soul. Then something picks the scab and opens the wound. The pain of grief comes pouring out, which may catch you off guard. Time may not totally heal the wound, but in time we learn to bandage it better. The cut will always run deep, but the bleeding will not always last as long.

Sometimes a grief relapse gently tugs on your heart strings for a few moments. At other times, the emotional pain can hit you like a ton of bricks. Don't try to understand it, just realize that it happens. Releasing the pressure valve of emotion is a natural aspect of soothing the soul.

Since confession is good for the soul, this author will readily admit that the subject of grief relapse was born out of personal experience. At the time of this writing, it has been nearly eight years since we lost our son, and the pain is still very present. Trust me, writing about grief relapse is not based on theory.

Writing about hope for the heavy heart is also not based on theory. I know that God provides hope through His Word. God says: "*For I know the thoughts that I think toward you, says the Lord, thoughts of peace and not of evil, to give you a future and a hope*" (Jeremiah 29:11). I can honestly say that the Lord delivers on His promise. He provides hope for the future, which gives us power in the present.

Jesus said: "*With men this is impossible, but with God all things are possible*" (Matthew 19:26). The Scripture also says: "*For with God nothing will be impossible*" (Luke 1:37). In other words, God specializes in things called impossible. After all, absolutely nothing is too difficult for God.

My friend, do not sell the power of God short. The Apostle Paul said: "*I can do all things through Christ who strengthens me*" (Philippians 4:13). The Lord will give you the inner strength to handle the deepest sorrow. When a grief relapse strikes at your soul, ask Christ to be your shield. The Lord will sustain you with His grace and give: Hope for your heavy heart.

19
Never Forgotten

Nobody wants their loved one to be forgotten. Their memory is always on your mind. Their love is always in your heart. Their spirit is always felt deep in your soul. They will never be forgotten by those who love them dearly.

Time stands still for nobody. The clock keeps ticking and the world keeps turning. The days turn into weeks, and weeks turn into months, and months turn into years. The calendar is a glaring reminder of the reality that time is marching on. In time, your loved one may become a distant memory to others, but they will never be forgotten by you.

Logic will never defeat love. Your mind knows they are gone, but your heart will never let go of their memory. You feel the presence of your loved one, as you look at photo albums, slide presentations, and home movies. Your heart skips a beat, as their pictures come to life.

A new calendar is created when you lose a loved one. Past events are looked upon as either, before or after, they passed away. Their death often becomes a filter for memories to be measured in life. It is possibly a subconscious way of guaranteeing that your loved one is never forgotten.

Fortunately, God never forgets us in our grief. God says: "*I will not forget you. See, I have inscribed you on the palms of My hands*" (Isaiah 49:15-16). This promise to Old Testament believers is repeated in the New Testament. Jesus said: "*I will never leave you nor forsake you*" (Hebrews 13:5). In other words, God's children are never forgotten by the Lord.

Jesus inscribed His love for us on the palms of His hands. Nails were driven into His hands when Christ died on the cross for our sins. His arms were outstretched with love, as Jesus cried out: "*Father, forgive them, for they do not know what they do*" (Luke 23:34).

Rest assured, when Christ was on the cross, you were on His mind. After Jesus rose from the dead, He gave the following promise: "*Lo, I am with you always, even to the end of the age*" (Matthew 28:20). Make no mistake about it, Jesus Christ always cares for His children.

David also affirmed God's love and care when he said: "*Yea, though I walk through the valley of the shadow of death, I will fear no evil; for You are with me; Your rod and your staff, they comfort me*" (Psalm 23:4). David sensed the presence of God during his darkest hour, which gave him peace in the valley.

My friend, the Savior has not forgotten about your sorrow. Jesus feels your pain and offers to carry your burden of grief. The Lord wants to walk with you, every step of the way, through your valley of the shadow of death. Just as your loved one will never be forgotten by you, the Lord will never forget to give: Hope for your heavy heart.

20
Where Do You Turn in a Time Like This?

You wish you could wake up from a bad dream. It is hard to believe it happened. It feels like time is standing still, as you watch yourself in slow motion. Your mind knows it has happened, but your broken heart does not want to accept that your loved one is gone.

Where do you turn in a time like this? The way you answer that question may make or break your future. This is a defining moment in your life. I believe the best direction to turn is toward the Lord. After all, the hope for your heavy heart is hanging in the balance.

The Scripture says: *"This is my comfort in my affliction, for Your word has given me life"* (Psalm 119:50). There are many artificial solutions, but only God can provide genuine comfort.

Psalm 55:22 says: *"Cast your burden on the Lord, and He shall sustain you; He shall never permit the righteous to be moved."* Pour out your heart to the Lord. God cares for you, and He promises to be the *"God of all comfort"* (II Corinthians 1:3).

Psalm 121:1-2 says: *"I will lift up my eyes to the hills - From whence comes my help? My help comes from the Lord, who made heaven and earth."* A healthy up-look is a valuable step for a hopeful outlook. The Creator is ready, willing, and able to give you comfort.

What can we learn in a time like this? First of all, remember the past. Cherish the precious memories of your loved one. Honor their life by reflecting on their memory with love.

Next, learn from the present. The Bible says: *"...life is like a vapor that appears for a little time and then vanishes away"* (James 4:14). Whether someone lives to a ripe old age, or has their life tragically cut short, in comparison to eternity, life is brief. It is like a puff of steam coming off the stove. It is here one moment, and gone the next. Life is too short to waste time on things that don't matter. Rebuild your life on the core values of: faith, family, and friends.

Finally, prepare for the future. Proverbs 27:1 says: *"Do not boast of tomorrow, for you do not know what a day may bring forth."* Life has no guarantees. Today is the best time to prepare for tomorrow. Affirm your faith in Christ. Tell Jesus that you believe He died and rose again for you.

My friend, I encourage you to turn to the Lord in prayer. You will be so glad you did. God will listen to the cry of your heart, and carry your burden of grief. Trust in Christ, and open your heart to His comfort. The compassion of Christ will give: Hope for your heavy heart.

21
Don't Lose Sight of the Living

Sorrow affects our sight. A broken heart blurs the vision of our eyes. The pain of death can blind us to people that still need us in their life. When we lose a loved one, we must keep in mind that other family members still need our love.

Don't lose sight of the living. People in your life still need your affirmation on their life. They long for your love and attention, but may be hesitant to let it show. They know you are hurting, so the last thing in the world they want to do is increase your burden.

It is crucial to not allow grief to rob you from loving the living. Taking the initiative to express your love to the people closest to you is very important. It is a valuable way of reassuring them of your desire to keep a vital relationship with them.

A couple of years after we lost our son, I wrote a letter to each of our children. I expressed my love and appreciation for them, and shared ways they were an inspiration to me. I wanted our living children to know that grief had not caused their Dad to lose sight of them. I presented the letter to each of them on Christmas Day.

I also used the occasion to express my love and appreciation to Cindi. I thanked her, in the presence of our children, for her courageous strength. It was a tender moment for the family. It brought tears to our eyes, warm hugs for one another, and gave hope to our heavy hearts.

In some ways, the occasion was also a tribute to Joseph. He brought so much joy to our family during his life. He would not want his death to cause us to lose sight of one another. I could almost see Joseph smiling down from heaven, in approval of his family, not losing sight of the living.

Jesus said: *"I am the resurrection and the life. He who believes in Me, though he may die, he shall live"* (John 11:25). The reality is that our loved ones, who are with the Lord, are more alive than ever before. They have simply gone before us, and are waiting for us to join them on the other side. We may be physically separated, but we are still spiritually connected through faith in Christ.

My friend, don't lose sight of the living. We may miss our loved ones in heaven, but we must not ignore our loved ones on earth. God wants us to encourage one another, and cheer each other on to the finish line. Affirm your love for the living, and the Lord will comfort you with: Hope for your heavy heart.

22
Honoring the Dignity of the Deceased

Respect is a noble character quality that honors the dignity of the deceased. After all, they are unable to defend themselves with a voice from the grave. The deceased rely on the loving loyalty of family and friends to uphold their dignity.

The Scripture says: *"And now abide faith, hope, love, these three; but the greatest of these is love"* (I Corinthians 13:13). Love affirms the strengths of people, and does not announce the shortcomings of human frailty. Love believes the best, gives the benefit of the doubt, and always honors the dignity of the deceased.

Sometimes a loved one may lose a battle in life, which contributed to their death. When such a tragedy occurs, a little discretion can go a long way. Honoring the dignity of the deceased is an act of discernment, not denial. It flows from a humble heart and a compassionate spirit.

Sadly, the gossip does not even respect the grave. They search for every speck of dirt in their shameless desire to sling mud. Refuse to give the self-righteous gossip any fuel for the fire.

Remember, your mission of mercy is to honor the noble memory of your loved one.

The nosy busybody will press you for information, but it is simply none of their business. You do not owe anyone any explanation. Never forget: People that really love you will not pry; and people that pry, do not really love you. True friends do not prey on you, they pray for you.

Ignore the insensitivity of thoughtless people. Do not allow their negativity to define the big picture of a positive life. Their callous perspective must not distract you from your compassionate purpose. Looking through the lens of love always succeeds because: *"Love never fails"* (I Corinthians 13:8).

The Golden Rule is the best way to honor the dignity of the deceased. Jesus said: *"Therefore, whatever you want men to do to you, do also to them, for this is the Law and the Prophets"* (Matthew 7:12). Treating people with respect is taking the high road in life. It is a display of Christian character, which includes honoring your loved one that is with the Lord.

My friend, it is a high calling to honor the dignity of the deceased. It is a great responsibility that requires compassion, courage, and conviction. This loving act of loyalty can also provide a boomerang blessing, as it circles back to give: Hope for your heavy heart.

23
Divine Help for Daily Hope

The loss of a loved one creates a hole in our heart, which cries out for hope. It is difficult to wrap our mind around the concept that our loved one is actually gone. We miss them dearly, and we think of them daily. As our heavy heart searches for comfort, reading the Twenty-Third Psalm, on a regular basis, can be a tremendous source of divine help for daily hope.

The Twenty-Third Psalm is truly one of the most comforting passages in all of Scripture. It says:

> *"The Lord is my Shepherd; I shall not want. He makes me to lie down in green pastures; He leads me beside the still waters. He restores my soul; He leads me in the paths of righteousness for His name's sake. Yea, though I walk through the valley of the shadow of death, I will fear no evil; For You are with me; Your rod and Your staff, they comfort me. You prepare a table before me in the presence of my enemies; You anoint my head with oil; My cup runs over. Surely goodness and mercy shall follow me all the days of my life; And I will dwell in the house of the Lord Forever"* (Psalm 23:1-6).

This beautiful Psalm could be called: Divine Help for Daily Hope. The encouraging words are very soothing to the soul. The inspirational message of the Twenty-Third Psalm provides a tremendous amount of hope for every heavy heart.

The image of the Lord caring for us like a loving shepherd is very comforting. The peaceful picture of His personal and tender care is very encouraging. The idea of His protection of our soul, and restoration of our inner spirit is very soothing. The eternal perspective of our heavenly home is very promising. Yes, the inspirational aspect of this divine help, offers us an incredible amount of daily hope.

The loss of hope can be seen in our physical appearance. Our head drops and our shoulders slump. The sparkle is gone, as our eyes lose their luster. Our smile fades, and our feet begin to shuffle.

Restored hope has the opposite effect. We hold our head high, as we walk, straight and tall, with our shoulders squared back. Our eyes sparkle, as our smile beams across our face. There is a fresh spring in our step, as we recapture our zest for life.

My friend, feast at the banqueting table of the Twenty-Third Psalm. It will inspire you with hope for the future, and power in the present. Hope is the momentum of life, and oxygen for the soul. The Lord, our Good Shepherd, graciously offers His divine help and a daily dose of: Hope for your heavy heart.

24
Soil Test of the Soul

The same sun that melts the ice, hardens the clay. The difference is not the sunshine, it is the soil. The same is true in our response to sorrow. Grief will become a soil test of the soul.

Guard your heart. The Scripture says: *"Keep your heart with all diligence, for out of it spring the issues of life"* (Proverbs 4:23). The heart is like a fountain. What you pour into it is what will flow out of it. Fill your mind with the love of God, and let hope spring from your heavy heart.

The heart is the control panel of your life. Everything goes through the switchboard of the heart, so keep the channel clear. Reject the negative attitude of resentment. Embrace the positive faith, which is built on the powerful truth that: *"With God all things are possible"* (Matthew 19:26).

One way to guard our heart is to avoid the dead end street called: If Only. It is a detour that only leads to further despair. Stay off the discouraging and depressing path of: If Only.

Another way to guard our heart is to resist the temptation of asking God why we lost a loved one. That question may never be answered this side of heaven. However, if we ask God what He wants to teach us, we will learn valuable life lessons from the adversity.

Beware of bitterness. It will color your thinking in an unhealthy way. The angry heart is a bad lens to view the loving hand of God. The hard heart is a bad filter to interpret the sustaining grace of God. Bitterness blinds our minds from seeing God's great faithfulness, during our most difficult circumstances of life.

Cultivate a tender heart and a teachable spirit. This will soften the soil of your soul. The Holy Spirit will plant the seed of the Word of God into the fertile ground of your heart. It will also help you hear the voice of God, as He whispers to you through His Word.

Reflect on The Lord's Prayer, which says:

"Our Father which art in heaven, Hallowed be Thy Name. Thy kingdom come. Thy will be done on earth, as it is in heaven. Give us this day our daily bread. And forgive us our debts (sins), as we forgive our debtors (those who sin against us). And lead us not into temptation, but deliver us from evil: For Thine is the kingdom, and the power, and the glory, forever. Amen" (Matthew 6:9-13, KJV).

Jesus taught this powerful prayer to His followers, and it has stood the test of time for all believers.

My friend, it takes a humble spirit to pass the soil test of the soul. In the classroom of life, God may use our loss to teach us in greater depth of His love. It is designed to make us better believers, not bitter doubters. Respond in faith and receive: Hope for your heavy heart.

25
The Sweet Sorrow of a Sad Good-Bye

It is very painful to watch a loved one suffer. You admire their courageous fight against a dreaded disease, but you know it is a losing battle. Some victories are not meant to be won this side of heaven. You know that it is only a matter of time, until you experience the sweet sorrow of a sad good-bye.

The family has gathered by the bedside, and hymns about heaven have been sung. Scriptures of comfort have been read, and a peaceful smile has come to your loved one's face. You cherish every moment together, as you say your final good-byes. You even tell them it is okay to go, as you grant them permission to go home to be with the Lord.

When the battle is finally over, it becomes the sweet sorrow of a sad good-bye. It is sad to say good-bye, but the sorrow is made sweeter because you know your loved one is out of pain. The helpless feeling of watching your loved one suffer in agony has finally come to a close. The Great Physician has decided to heal your loved one in heaven.

There is almost a sense of relief in knowing the battle on earth is finished. Your loved one has left this world, and has been welcomed into the arms of the Lord. The victory is boldly proclaimed when your loved one steps into their home in heaven.

The Scripture says the following about heaven: *"And God will wipe away every tear from their eyes; there shall be no more death, nor sorrow, nor crying; and there shall be no more pain, for the former things have passed away"* (Revelation 21:4).

Heaven is a real place for real people. There will not be any sorrow, no pain, and no suffering in heaven. No sad good-byes, no broken hearts, and no tears streaming down our face. Heaven is a peaceful place, filled with comfort and joy.

Heaven is a beautiful paradise. The family of God will gather beside the river of life. The walls of jasper will glisten, as we walk together on the streets of gold. The Lord will be the light of heaven, and His love will be the talk of the town.

My friend, take comfort in the sweet sorrow of a sad good-bye. It is not a final farewell to your loved one. It is a temporary parting on earth, but a permanent reunion is waiting in heaven. It is sweet to know their pain is over, and your sad sorrow will not last forever. Keep the faith, and the Lord will give: Hope for your heavy heart.

26
Precious in the Sight of the Lord

The Scripture says: *"Precious in the sight of the Lord is the death of His saints"* (Psalm 116:15). In Scripture, a saint is simply another title for a believer. The idea is that the Lord takes a special interest in calling one of His children home to heaven.

The New Testament reveals three precious metaphors for death, which are designed to comfort a believer. The first one is "falling asleep." The Bible says: *"But I do not want you to be unaware, brethren, concerning those who have fallen asleep, lest you sorrow as others who have no hope"* (I Thessalonians 4:13).

Sleep is a picture of peace. Someone that is sleeping has a peaceful look on their face. As believers in Christ, we have peace with God, and the peace of God.

The next metaphor is "going on a journey." Near the end of his life, the Apostle Paul said: *"The time of my departure is at hand"* (II Timothy 4:6). The word "departure" gives the idea of untying a boat to set sail, or loosening a tent to break camp. This is a picture of preparation. The believer in Christ has their bags packed, and they are ready to go on a journey with the Lord.

The Lord gave a third metaphor for death in the New Testament when He said: *"In My Father's house are many mansions; if it were not so, I would have told you. I go to prepare a place for you. And if I go and prepare a place for you, I will come again and receive you to Myself; that where I am, there you may be also"* (John 14:2-3).

This is a picture of going home. It is always pleasant to go home. Like the old saying goes: There is no place like home. Our loved one has gone home to be with the Lord.

My friend, the three precious metaphors for death in the New Testament provide comfort in life. It is encouraging to know that we will see our loved ones again. They have fallen asleep, and have gone on a journey, and have safely arrived at their eternal home. Looking forward to that sweet reunion, on the beautiful shores of heaven, will give: Hope for your heavy heart.

27
Sorrow is Scriptural

Tears are the reality of love, not the result of a lack of faith. Tears are a symbol of a strong bond, not a sign of a weak believer. The pain of losing a loved one goes well below the surface of our soul. It is natural for the deep well of emotion to occasionally bubble over from our broken heart.

If you were raised in an old school environment, you may feel uncomfortable with any display of emotion. Particularly, revealing the sorrow that grips your grieving soul. The idea of keeping a stiff upper lip is contrary to the reality of a broken heart. Therefore, it can be helpful to have a place where you can grieve privately and release your emotions openly.

Two of the most powerful words in Scripture are found in John 11:35, where the Bible says: "*Jesus wept.*" This proves that sorrow is Scriptural because Jesus is the sinless Son of God. Christ was deeply moved with heart-felt sorrow at the death of His very close friend, Lazarus. It caused the Lord to openly weep at the pain and suffering of the loss of life. The word picture of "*wept*" is the idea of Jesus having tears streaming down His face, not simply misty eyes.

The compassionate tears of Christ caused the people to say: *"See how He loved him!"* (John 11:36). The tears of Jesus were a demonstration of great love, not a declaration of a lack of faith. The Gospel of John goes on to paint a vivid picture of Jesus, the perfect God-Man. As a human being, Jesus was broken hearted over the loss of His friend. As God, Jesus boldly walked into the tomb-like cave, and raised Lazarus bodily from the dead (John 11:38-44).

Jesus is the ultimate hope for every heavy heart. His love and compassion for our pain and suffering is a source of great comfort. His open display of genuine grief is the best example for us to not be ashamed of our hurting heart. Our human frailty is not a sign of weakness, it is a symbol of the strong love we have in our heart for the one we lost.

The Bible says that we are: *"created in the image of God"* (Genesis 1:27). In other words, we have a mind to think, emotions to feel, and a will to choose. God created us with an emotional component, and the Son of God demonstrated emotional compassion. Therefore, we should not consider it shameful to express our sorrow (especially in private). Releasing tears behind the scenes is like releasing the valve on a pressure cooker. It lets out the steam privately, which helps avoid a public meltdown.

My friend, if Jesus Christ wept over the loss of a loved one, then we can weep too. Tears are a sign of deep love, not shallow faith. Sorrow is Scriptural, so pour out your pain to the Lord, and He will provide: Hope for your heavy heart.

28
Permission to Laugh

Sorrow and laughter are like oil and water. They simply do not mix. It is very difficult to put on a happy face when a dagger has been put through your heart. Your misty eyes blur your vision, as you search for your smile. The grief that grips your heart, refuses to let go. My friend, in time you simply have to give yourself permission to laugh.

A couple of months after we lost Joseph, our son Jacob shipped out for a tour of duty with the United States Marine Corps. With heavy hearts we said good-bye, and we prayed earnestly that God would bring him home safely. We were very thankful when the good Lord brought our son home safe and sound.

When my wife and I boarded the plane to fly out to greet our son, I told Cindi that we were going to give ourselves permission to laugh. Jacob had bravely served his country for nine months in an overseas mission with the USMC. Our son needed to see his parents smile again.

Cindi and I were all smiles as we greeted Jacob when he stepped off the ship. It was a happy reunion filled warm hugs and big smiles. The laughter on our lips reflected the joy in our hearts. If there were any tears at that moment, they were tears of joy.

I rented a house on the beach so we could enjoy some quality time together. We were thrilled to see Jacob and it was great to relax with him. Whether we were sharing a meal, playing cards, or just shooting the breeze, we made sure there was plenty of laughter in the air.

When we returned home, we decided to brighten the house with our new found smile. Our daughter Hannah, who was still living at home, undoubtedly found it to be a breath of fresh air. Later at the office, I told our son Michael about my decision to give ourselves permission to laugh. He grinned and stated that Jacob had called him during our visit and said: "Dad was smiling and seemed to be having a good time."

My instincts had been right. Our children needed to see their parents smiling again. It was a symbol of hope on the horizon. It was a sign that it was still okay for our family to have a little fun. Our resurrected enjoyment for life had encouraged their heavy hearts with hope. It was also a tribute to our son in heaven. Joseph brought so much laughter to our family when he was living, he would not want his passing to destroy the spirit of joy in our home.

The Scripture says: *"A merry heart does good like medicine, but a broken spirit dries the bones"* (Proverbs 17:22). Laughter is truly good for the soul. It is like a shot of inspiration for the human spirit. The opposite is also true. The loss of laughter brings a pain that runs so deep, it is felt clear down into the bones. Sometimes, laughter can be the best medicine for your soul.

My friend, give yourself permission to laugh. The Scriptural prescription of laughter can revive your spirit, and refresh others close to you. Healthy laughter brings relief from pain, and offers the healing balm of: Hope for your heavy heart.

29
Body, Soul, and Spirit

The doctor in the Emergency Room looked me square in the eye and said: "Mike, you dodged a bullet today." He went on to say that: "Somebody upstairs was watching out for you." I told him that I had a son in heaven, and maybe my son had put in a good word to the Lord for me. I could almost hear Joseph say: "Lord, if you don't mind, give my Dad a break."

My blood pressure was in a dangerous zone when we arrived at the hospital. They quickly went to work to bring my blood pressure down. We had flown to California for the birth of our granddaughter, and the next thing I knew, I was in the hospital.

It all started when I went to shave that morning in our hotel room. The right side of my face felt tingly. I reached for the razor, and my right hand felt numb. I decided to sit down on the couch, and my right foot felt like it had fallen asleep. My body was sending me a strange signal.

I told my wife what was happening, and she wanted to take me to the ER immediately. The tingling had subsided, so I decided to phone a doctor friend back home in Indiana. When I told him my symptoms, he instructed me to go to the nearest hospital right away. I tried to reason with him, but the doctor insisted, and we did as instructed.

At the ER in California, I told the doctor that I had probably internalized my grief. I asked him if that could have any bearing on my blood pressure. He assured me that it could. Then the doctor told me to: lose weight, exercise vigorously, and lose the salt shaker. It was my wake-up call. I realized that I had much to live for, and my family needed me.

I started walking on the treadmill, and changed my eating habits. I made sensible food substitutions (fresh fruit instead of French fries). I listened to positive motivation while walking, which I called my Treadmill University. In time, I became a devout believer in the connection of the body, soul, and spirit. The weight came off, my blood pressure went down, and I felt better. It literally developed into my own personal grief therapy.

The Scripture says: *"Now may the God of peace Himself sanctify you completely; and may your whole, spirit, soul, and body be preserved blameless at the coming of our Lord Jesus Christ"* (I Thessalonians 5:23). There is a strong connection between our physical body, emotional spirit, and spiritual soul. When all three aspects of life are guided by the Lord, God gives us an inner peace.

My friend, there is great value in a healthy lifestyle. Take small steps to improve your physical, emotional, and spiritual life. Little things can make a big difference on the road to recovery. God blesses a balanced life with peace of mind and: Hope for your heavy heart.

30
Flock Together with Birds of a Feather

Handling deep sorrow in a shallow culture is not easy. Many people are uncomfortable being around someone that has lost a loved one. They might attend the viewing and funeral, but after that, grief becomes a closed subject.

As you face death in a culture of life, there can be some awkward moments. You mention the loss of your loved one to a friend, and it might fall on deaf ears. They may even change the subject, right in the middle of your sentence. It seems insensitive, but it is just their way of sending a signal of their uneasiness about your grief.

You may need to look for some birds of a feather and flock together. A support group can be a helpful way to handle your grief. Having a listening ear, in a compassionate setting, is worth its weight in gold. It is a priceless gift to know that you are not alone.

There is a bond in brokenness. It is encouraging to gather with others that understand how you feel. They can empathize with your heavy heart. They know the importance of allowing you to talk openly about the pain of losing a loved one. They would never dream of changing the subject, as you share cherished memories, and precious moments of the past.

The Scripture says: *"Bear one another's burdens, and so fulfill the law of Christ"* (Galatians 6:2). Hanging out with others, that share a common need of comfort, is a beautiful way to share the love of Christ. The walking wounded need a shoulder to lean on because the burden is so great. Your presence in the group will also encourage someone else in their grief.

The Scripture says: *"A friend loves at all times, and a brother is born for adversity"* (Proverbs 17:17). If old friends are hard to find, it may be time to find some new ones. A grief support group can be a good place to look. Your common bond of brokenness will give you a mutual understanding of one another. Grief can be a glue that holds new friendships together.

My friend, your constant companion of grief is shared by many others. There are plenty of hurting people traveling with you on the lonely road of adversity. You might consider starting your own grief support network. If this book has been helpful, I would be honored if you used it as a group discussion guide. Most importantly, don't walk alone. Flock together with birds of a feather, and the Lord will give: Hope for your heavy heart.

31
The God of All Comfort

God is called the *"God of all comfort"* and He lives up to His title (II Corinthians 1:3). God comforts us with His presence. The Scripture says: *"You will show me the path of life; in Your presence is fullness and joy; at Your right hand are pleasures forevermore"* (Psalm 16:11). God's presence in our journey of sorrow brings joy to our soul. It is simply good to know that the loving hand of God is supporting our heavy heart of grief.

God also comforts us with His people. The Scripture instructs us to: *"Weep with those who weep"* (Romans 12:15). The Lord uses the family of God to be an extension of His love. It is comforting to know that God does not want us to suffer alone. Our loving Savior wraps His arms around us through the hugs of His people that feel our pain.

During the viewing and funeral of our son, countless people extended their love to us. One that stands out in particular is our Uncle Vic. When he and Aunt Becky came through the receiving line, our son Jacob thanked them for attending. Uncle Vic hugged Jacob and said: "You don't have to thank family. This is what family does." It made a lasting impression on Jacob, and meant the world to our entire family.

Some of our friends became like family during our darkest hour. They supported us with hugs, prayers, and loving kindness. After the funeral, I stated to our family and close friends: "Family is more than flesh and blood, and you don't have to be flesh and blood to be family."

God also comforts us with His promises. The Psalmist said: *"This is my comfort in my affliction, for Your word has given me life"* (Psalm 119:50). The promises of the Word of God inspire our heart with hope. When our life is shaped by suffering, our faith does not suffer shipwreck. The promises of God provide peace of mind in the midst of the storms of life.

Jesus said: *"I am the resurrection and the life. He who believes in Me, though he may die, he (or she) shall live"* (John 11:25). The promise of the resurrection gives us hope for the future, and power in the present. It is a tremendous source of strength to know that we will see our loved ones again.

It is comforting to know that our believing loved ones are with the Lord. The Bible says: *"We are confident, yes, well pleased rather to be absent from the body and to be present with the Lord"* (II Corinthians 5:8). Make no mistake about it, the Scriptures are very clear about eternal life. The believer in Jesus Christ goes straight to heaven after they take their last breath on earth.

My friend, God comforts us with His presence, His people, and His promises. God offers the ultimate promise of eternal life to anyone that invites Christ into their life. Affirm your faith in Christ, and experience the peaceful, easy feeling of His love. Receive the free gift of eternal life, and the God of all comfort will give: Hope for your heavy heart.

32
Hang on to Hope

The loss of a loved one can flood our soul with sorrow. The painful despair can intensify if we are not sure of what they believed. Therefore, I would like to offer several reasons why our faith can hang on to hope.

First and foremost, the love of God is extended to the entire human race. Jesus said: *"For God so loved the world that He gave His only begotten Son, that whoever believes in Him should not perish but have everlasting life"* (John 3:16). Jesus Christ put the unconditional and universal love of God on display at the cross, and He invites everyone to believe.

We also know that God wants everyone to trust Christ as Savior. The Scripture says: *"For this is good and acceptable in the sight of God our Savior, who desires all men to be saved and to come to the knowledge of the truth"* (I Timothy 2:3-4). Rest assured, God has made it possible for heaven to be very well populated.

The Word of God also indicates that humanity has an eternal awareness. The Lord tells us that: *"He has put eternity in their hearts"* (Ecclesiastes 3:11). God has given human beings an instinctive insight on eternity. One never knows the way a

God-given spiritual instinct plays out in the final moments of life.

Another possibility is that your loved one may have trusted Christ, and never told you. They may have learned about the love of Christ as a child at a Vacation Bible School. They could have also heard the good news of the gospel from a classmate, teammate, co-worker, neighbor, or friend. They might have tuned in to a preacher of the gospel on the radio or TV. It is even possible that a total stranger handed them a gospel tract, and after reading it, they trusted Christ.

The Lord also reveals Himself in nature. The Bible says: "*The heavens declare the glory of God*" (Psalm 19:1). Your loved one may have looked up at the stars, and realized there is a higher power. This may have motivated them to search a little further in their quest for truth.

The Lord also reveals Himself through the Scriptures. Jesus said: "*the Scriptures testify of Christ*" (John 5:39). Curiosity may have led your loved one to read about Christ in the four Gospels. As a result, they may have quietly responded with faith in the risen Lord.

It is even being reported that people, in non-Christian countries, are having dreams about the death, burial, and resurrection of Christ. The Lord is supernaturally revealing Himself through these dreams, and many are responding with faith in Christ. It is an incredible example of the amazing grace of God.

My friend, hang on to hope. You never know what happens in the final moments of life. God can grant the gift of eternal life when someone is taking their final breath. Cling to the love of Christ, and trust His mercy to give: Hope for your heavy heart.

33
Grace in the Midst of Gethsemane

The Garden of Gethsemane is where Jesus wrestled with His destiny. At Gethsemane, Christ came to terms with the role of agony on the road to victory. The cross was a "bitter cup" that weighed heavily on the mind of Christ. The success of the resurrection included the suffering of the crucifixion, and the sorrow of Gethsemane. In the Garden, the Son prayed with great intensity, and the Father provided Grace in the midst of Gethsemane.

The Gospel of Mark describes the agonizing scene as follows:

> *"Then they came to a place which was named Gethsemane; and He said to His disciples, 'Sit here while I pray.' And He took Peter, James, and John with Him, and He began to be troubled and deeply distressed. Then He said to them, 'My soul is exceedingly sorrowful, even to death. Stay here and watch.' He went a little farther, and fell on the ground, and prayed that if it were possible, the hour might pass from Him. And He said, 'Abba, Father, all things are possible for You. Take this cup away from Me; nevertheless, not what I will, but what You will.' Then He came and found them sleeping, and said to Peter, 'Simon, are you*

sleeping? Could you not watch one hour?'" (Mark 14:32-37).

This pattern was repeated three times. Christ, in great agony, would pour out His heart to the Father. Then He would return to His close friends, and find them sleeping, instead of praying. The Gospel of Luke tells us that Christ prayed with such intensity that His sweat became like great drops of blood falling to the ground. Fortunately, an angel appeared to Christ and strengthened Him (Luke 22:43-45).

I believe that losing a loved one brings us to our own Gethsemane experience. It is a very painful cross to bear. It forces us to drink from the bitter cup of immense sorrow. With a heavy heart, we all search for Grace in the Midst of Gethsemane.

I will never forget the moment when the paramedic looked up and said: "I am sorry, we did all that we could do." Time stood still, as I felt the crushing blow of overwhelming sorrow. I dropped to my knees, gathered my lifeless son into my arms, and gently kissed him on the cheek.

My friend, the Gethsemane experience is deeply personal. It is between you and God. Even Jesus faced it alone. Christ wanted His friends to support Him, but they were asleep when He needed them the most. If you feel like your friends have abandoned you, don't be too hard on them. God wants to be your personal comfort in your private Gethsemane. Pour out your heavy heart to the Lord, and He will give you the grace to endure the hardship.

The Gethsemane experience is also unbearably painful. The idea behind the pain that Christ endured is a concept of sorrow that is almost suffocating. The grief is so intense that it literally has a person gasping for air. I know you get the picture. I am confident that you can identify with the type of sorrow that takes your breath away.

The heartbreak of losing a loved one can make us feel as if: The world stops turning; the sun stops shining; the breeze stops blowing; the birds stop singing; the music stops playing; the laughter stops ringing; our friends stop calling; our eyes stop sparkling, and our smile starts fading. All because our heart keeps on breaking.

However, in the midst of the pain, God is still listening. God is still working. God is still caring because God is still loving. The comforting hand of God will uphold your heavy heart.

The Gethsemane experience is also distinctly pivotal. Your life will never be the same. This pivotal moment in time becomes a turning point in life. Quite frankly, it can either make us bitter doubters, or better believers. If we blame God, it will lead to bitterness. However, if we trust God, it will affirm our faith, as we allow the Lord to guide our painful journey.

The Gethsemane experience can also be spiritually profitable. Our total dependence on God causes us to draw closer to the Lord, which strengthens our faith. You see, when the will of God becomes all that matters, your walk with God will take on an entirely new meaning. Also, when the cross you bear brings glory to God, your light will shine brightly on the cross of Christ.

In that painful moment when I held our lifeless son in my arms, I felt the Lord's presence in a very personal way. I sensed the Lord saying that He was going to take me through the darkest time of my life. However, when the fog lifted, I would discover my greatest ministry. I experienced God's comfort, and His sustaining grace in that moment of incredible heartbreak.

I can honestly say that it would not have been my game plan for ministry, but God has used our loss to comfort many others. We have seen our pain become a platform for the good news of the gospel. Countless people have placed their faith in Christ because they observed His Grace in the Midst of our Gethsemane. This does not eliminate our pain, but it does provide a tremendous sense of purpose for our pain. We give God the glory for His great faithfulness.

My friend, keep your faith in the Lord. In time, the world will start turning, the sun will start shining, and you will feel the breeze begin to blow. You will hear the birds singing, the music playing, and the laughter ringing. Eventually, new friends will be calling, your eyes will be sparkling, and a beaming smile will cover your face. Your broken heart may not completely heal this side of heaven, but God can restore a spirit of joy for the journey. God loves you, and He will give Grace in the Midst of your Gethsemane, along with: Hope for your heavy heart.

34
Hope on the Horizon

Faith anticipates life after death. The grave is not the end of the story for the believer. The promise of a future reunion brings an inner peace to the present reality. The truth that we will see our loved ones again, inspires our heavy heart with hope.

The New Testament describes our Hope on the Horizon as follows:

> "Behold, I tell you a mystery: We shall not all sleep, but we shall all be changed; in a moment, in the twinkling of an eye, at the last trumpet. For the trumpet will sound, and the dead will be raised incorruptible, and we shall be changed. For this corruptible must put on incorruption, and this mortal must put on immortality. So when this corruptible has put on incorruption, and this mortal has put on immortality, then shall be brought to pass the saying that is written: 'Death is swallowed up in victory.' O Death, where is your sting? O Hades, where is your victory? The sting of death is sin, and the strength of sin is the law. But thanks be to God, who gives us the victory through our Lord Jesus Christ" (I Corinthians 15:51-57).

The Resurrection of Jesus Christ gives us Hope on the Horizon. The empty tomb of Christ defeated our greatest enemy called death. His resurrection guarantees our resurrection. The triumph of Christ over death is the reason we believe in eternal life.

The word *"behold"* is a spotlight word. God is literally shining His spotlight on our: Hope on the Horizon. He is reminding us of our victory over the grave. The resurrection of Christ is proof that we are on the winning team.

The Return of Christ also gives us: Hope on the Horizon. The *"twinkling of an eye"* means the Return of Christ is imminent. It could happen at any moment. The *"sounding of the trumpet"* is a word picture of a wake-up call. Just like the military has a trumpet reveille to announce the dawning of a new day, God will announce His new day with a trumpet blast.

Our Reunion with Christ, and all of His followers, gives us Hope on the Horizon. One day we will be reunited with our loved ones in heaven. In a parallel passage on the resurrection of believers, at the Return of Christ, God tells us to: *"comfort one another with these words"* (I Thessalonians 4:18). It is very comforting to know that we will see our loved ones again.

My friend, keep on, keeping on. There is Hope on the Horizon. Keep a listening ear for the trumpet of God, and a watchful eye for the Return of Christ. This will give you the strength to keep: Soldiering on for the Savior. One day, we will be reunited with our loved ones. This beautiful truth will bless your life with: Hope for your heavy heart.

35
Hope for Every Heart

The love of God offers hope for every heart. The Scripture says: *"For God so loved the world that He gave His only begotten Son, that whoever believes in Him should not perish but have everlasting life"* (John 3:16). God loves the entire human race, and He offers the free gift of eternal life to all who believe.

The desire of God to rescue humanity gives hope for every heart. The Scripture says: *"For this is good and acceptable in the sight of God our Savior, who desires all men (all people) to be saved and to come to the knowledge of the truth"* (I Timothy 2:3-4). The truth is that God wants everyone to accept Christ as Savior.

The good news of the gospel gives hope for every heart. The Scripture says that: *"...Christ died for our sins according to the Scriptures, and that He was buried, and that He rose again the third day according to the Scriptures"* (I Corinthians 15:3-4). The resurrection of Jesus Christ is the greatest event in human history, and the best news in the world.

The divine solution for the human sin problem gives hope for every heart. The Scripture says: *"For all have sinned and fall short of the glory of God"* (Romans 3:23). Sin separates us from God, but that is not the end of the story. The Scripture says: *"But God demonstrates His own love toward us, in that while we were still sinners, Christ died for us"* (Romans 5:8). Christ built the bridge at the cross in order to connect us to God.

Two thousand years ago, God stepped out of heaven in the Person of Jesus Christ. He was born of the Virgin, and lived a sinless life. Christ died on the cross, as a sacrifice for our sins, and bodily resurrected from the dead. His victory over the grave gives hope for every heart.

The gift of salvation, by grace through faith, gives hope for every heart. The Scripture says: *"For by grace you have been saved through faith, and that not of yourselves; it is the gift of God, not of works, lest anyone should boast"* (Ephesians 2:8-9). Grace is the love of God in action for you. Faith is total trust in the Lord Jesus Christ, as your personal Savior.

There is hope for every heart that takes their faith from a formal religion about Christ, to a personal relationship with Christ. You can affirm your faith in Christ by praying the following:

> Dear God, I thank You for sending Your Son to be my Savior. I believe that Jesus Christ died on the cross and bodily rose again for my sins. I invite Christ into my life to be my personal Lord and Savior. Thank You for dying for me. Help me to live for You. In Jesus' Name, Amen.

My friend, God understands the universal human need of hope. After all, in the circle of life, everybody loses somebody. I pray that the God of all comfort will give hope to every heart. I trust that God will sustain all hurting people with His grace, and guard their hearts with His peace. It is my sincere desire that the incredible love of God, the infinite mercy of Christ, and the inspirational power of the Holy Spirit will provide: Hope for every heavy heart.

My friend, if you prayed to invite Christ into your life, please let us know.

Thank you and God Bless You.

Power for Living Ministry
P.O. Box 4396
South Bend, IN 46634

Email: pflmike@aol.com

www.powerforlivingministry.com

About The Author

Dr. Michael A. Cramer is the founder of the Power for Living Ministry. He is a gifted communicator and inspirational leader. Mike believes in a positive faith, which embraces the powerful truth that: *with God all things are possible.* His emphasis on positive faith encourages people from all walks of life, and connects with leaders in the faith, business, and athletic communities. For more than three decades, Mike has also served as Senior Pastor of New Life Church in Osceola, IN. His motivational speaking, inspirational books, and radio broadcast have expanded the ministry far beyond the borders of New Life. Mike is richly blessed to have his beautiful and loving wife, Cindi, at his side. As parents, they have faced the agonizing pain of losing their twenty-eight year old son. As ministry partners, they have walked through the valley of grief with countless hurting families. They have the credibility and compassion to comfort the walking wounded. Mike and Cindi have four children (Joseph is with the Lord) and seven grandchildren.

Educational Background:

D.Min., Grace Theological Seminary, Winona Lake, IN
M.A., Moody Bible Institute, Chicago, IL
B.A., Bethel College, Mishawaka, IN
Diploma, Word of Life Bible Institute, Schroon Lake, NY

Seminars by Dr. Michael A. Cramer

Mike offers valuable insights on: Effective Ministry, Motivating Men, Marriage Matters, Dynamic Leadership, and Facing Grief.

OTHER BOOKS BY DR. MICHAEL A. CRAMER

Power Moments

Fifty-two short chapters of positive motivation and powerful inspiration. It encourages believers, builds a bridge to seekers, and motivates winners in the game of life.

Power Moments **is also available in Spanish.**

Fireside Chats to Fire Up Churches

Twenty short chapters of proven principles for an effective ministry. It is not a "how to" book on church growth, but a helpful tool for developing a healthy ministry.

Dynamics of Effective Leadership Development

A twelve-session Bible study guide on the foundational values for effective ministry.

Special Recognition

Power for Living wishes to recognize Dr. Kelly Carr, founder of Franklin Publishing in Princeton, Texas. His professional and personal service is outstanding. For any of your publishing needs, we highly recommend you visit:
www.FranklinPublishing.org

Power for Living Purpose

The Purpose of the Power for Living Ministry is to communicate a positive Christian message and empower people to achieve success through the motivational and inspirational teaching of sacred truth. www.PowerForLivingMinistry.com

ORDER FORM

Additional Copies of **Hope For The Heavy Heart:**

One (1 copy), suggested donation: $10.00

Five (5 copies), suggested donation: $35.00

Ten (10 copies), suggested donation: $60.00

An encouraging gift for grieving family & friends.
(Order 5 copies & save 30%))

An excellent resource for a grief support group.
(Order 10 copies & save 40%)

All orders include the cost of shipping.

Please make checks payable to *Power for Living Ministry* and mail to:

Power for Living Ministry
P.O. Box 4396
South Bend, IN 46634

Email: pflmike@aol.com

www.PowerforLivingMinistry.com

Thank you for helping us share the positive faith, which embraces the powerful truth that:

"With God all things are possible."

Now May The Lord Bless You and Keep You.

May The Lord Shine His Love Upon You.

May The Lord Comfort You with His Mercy

And Sustain You with His Grace.

May The Lord Give You Peace of Mind

And Hold You in the Palm of His Hand.

May The Lord Give You Power for Living

And Hope for Your Heavy Heart. Amen.

God Bless You,
Mike and Cindi Cramer

NAT TURNER

NAT TURNER

❦

Terry Bisson

Senior Consulting Editor
Nathan Irvin Huggins
Director
*W.E.B. Du Bois Institute for Afro-American Research
Harvard University*

CHELSEA HOUSE PUBLISHERS
Philadelphia

Chelsea House Publishers

Editor-in-Chief   Nancy Toff
Executive Editor   Remmel T. Nunn
Managing Editor   Karyn Gullen Browne
Copy Chief   Juliann Barbato
Picture Editor   Adrian G. Allen
Art Director   Giannella Garrett
Manufacturing Manager   Gerald Levine

Black Americans of Achievement

Senior Editor   Richard Rennert

Staff for NAT TURNER

Associate Editor   Perry King
Assistant Editor   Gillian Bucky
Copy Editor   Karen Hammonds
Deputy Copy Chief   Ellen Scordato
Editorial Assistant   Susan DeRosa
Associate Picture Editor   Juliette Dickstein
Picture Researcher   Toby Greenberg
Senior Designer   Laurie Jewell
Design Assistant   Laura Lang
Production Coordinator   Joseph Romano
Cover Illustration   Alan J. Nahigian

15 14 13

Library of Congress Cataloging in Publication Data

Bisson, Terry.
  Nat Turner.

  (Black Americans of Achievement)
  Includes index.
  Summary: A biography of the slave and preacher who, believing that God wanted him to free the slaves, led a major
revolt in 1831.
    1. Turner, Nat, 1800?–1831—Juvenile literature.
  2. Slaves—Virginia—Biography—Juvenile literature.
  3. Southampton Insurrection, 1831—Juvenile literature.
  [1. Turner, Nat, 1800?–1831.   2. Slaves.
  3. Afro-Americans—Biography]   I. Title.   II. Series.
  F232.S7T873   1988   975.5'5503'0924 [B] [92]
  87-37559
  ISBN 1-55546-613-3

     0-7910-0214-4   (pbk.)

CONTENTS

BLACK AMERICANS OF ACHIEVEMENT

HENRY AARON
baseball great

KAREEM ABDUL-JABBAR
basketball great

MUHAMMAD ALI
heavyweight champion

RICHARD ALLEN
*religious leader and
social activist*

MAYA ANGELOU
author

LOUIS ARMSTRONG
musician

ARTHUR ASHE
tennis great

JOSEPHINE BAKER
entertainer

JAMES BALDWIN
author

TYRA BANKS
model

BENJAMIN BANNEKER
scientist and mathematician

AMIRI BARAKA
poet and playwright

COUNT BASIE
bandleader and composer

ROMARE BEARDEN
artist

JAMES BECKWOURTH
frontiersman

MARY MCLEOD BETHUNE
educator

GEORGE WASHINGTON
CARVER
botanist

CHARLES CHESNUTT
author

JOHNNIE COCHRAN
lawyer

BILL COSBY
entertainer

PAUL CUFFE
merchant and abolitionist

MILES DAVIS
musician

FATHER DIVINE
religious leader

FREDERICK DOUGLASS
abolitionist editor

CHARLES DREW
physician

W. E. B. DU BOIS
scholar and activist

PAUL LAURENCE DUNBAR
poet

DUKE ELLINGTON
bandleader and composer

RALPH ELLISON
author

JULIUS ERVING
basketball great

LOUIS FARRAKHAN
political activist

ELLA FITZGERALD
singer

MORGAN FREEMAN
actor

MARCUS GARVEY
black nationalist leader

JOSH GIBSON
baseball great

WHOOPI GOLDBERG
entertainer

CUBA GOODING JR.
actor

ALEX HALEY
author

PRINCE HALL
social reformer

JIMI HENDRIX
musician

MATTHEW HENSON
explorer

GREGORY HINES
performer

BILLIE HOLIDAY
singer

LENA HORNE
entertainer

WHITNEY HOUSTON
singer and actress

LANGSTON HUGHES
poet

ZORA NEALE HURSTON
author

JANET JACKSON
singer

JESSE JACKSON
civil-rights leader and politician

MICHAEL JACKSON
entertainer

SAMUEL L. JACKSON
actor

T. D. JAKES
religious leader

JACK JOHNSON
heavyweight champion

MAGIC JOHNSON
basketball great

SCOTT JOPLIN
composer

BARBARA JORDAN
politician

MICHAEL JORDAN
basketball great

CORETTA SCOTT KING
civil-rights leader

MARTIN LUTHER KING JR.
civil-rights leader

LEWIS LATIMER
scientist

SPIKE LEE
filmmaker

CARL LEWIS
champion athlete

JOE LOUIS
heavyweight champion

RONALD MCNAIR
astronaut

MALCOLM X
militant black leader

BOB MARLEY
musician

THURGOOD MARSHALL
Supreme Court justice

TONI MORRISON
author

ELIJAH MUHAMMAD
religious leader

EDDIE MURPHY
entertainer

JESSE OWENS
champion athlete

SATCHEL PAIGE
baseball great

CHARLIE PARKER
musician

ROSA PARKS
civil-rights leader

COLIN POWELL
military leader

PAUL ROBESON
singer and actor

JACKIE ROBINSON
baseball great

CHRIS ROCK
comedian/actor

DIANA ROSS
entertainer

WILL SMITH
actor

CLARENCE THOMAS
Supreme Court justice

SOJOURNER TRUTH
antislavery activist

HARRIET TUBMAN
antislavery activist

NAT TURNER
slave revolt leader

TINA TURNER
entertainer

DENMARK VESEY
slave revolt leader

ALICE WALKER
author

MADAM C. J. WALKER
entrepreneur

BOOKER T. WASHINGTON
educator

DENZEL WASHINGTON
actor

J. C. WATTS
politician

VANESSA WILLIAMS
singer and actress

OPRAH WINFREY
entertainer

TIGER WOODS
golf star

RICHARD WRIGHT
author

ON
ACHIEVEMENT

——— ❧ ———

Coretta Scott King

BEFORE YOU BEGIN this book, I hope you will ask yourself what the word excellence means to you. I think that it's a question we should all ask, and keep asking as we grow older and change. Because the truest answer to it should never change. When you think of excellence, perhaps you think of success at work; or of becoming wealthy; or meeting the right person, getting married, and having a good family life.

Those important goals are worth striving for, but there is a better way to look at excellence. As Martin Luther King, Jr., said in one of his last sermons, "I want you to be first in love. I want you to be first in moral excellence. I want you to be first in generosity. If you want to be important, wonderful. If you want to be great, wonderful. But recognize that he who is greatest among you shall be your servant."

My husband, Martin Luther King, Jr., knew that the true meaning of achievement is service. When I met him, in 1952, he was already ordained as a Baptist preacher and was working towards a doctoral degree at Boston University. I was studying at the New England Conservatory and dreamed of accomplishments in music. We married a year later, and after I graduated the following year we moved to Montgomery, Alabama. We didn't know it then, but our notions of achievement were about to undergo a dramatic change.

You may have read or heard about what happened next. What began with the boycott of a local bus line grew into a national movement, and by the time he was assassinated in 1968 my husband had fashioned a black movement powerful enough to shatter forever the practice of racial segregation. What you may not have read about is where he got his method for resisting injustice without compromising his religious beliefs.

He got the strategy of nonviolence from a man of a different race, who lived in a distant country, and even practiced a different religion. The man was Mahatma Gandhi, the great leader of India, who devoted his life to serving humanity in the spirit of love and nonviolence. It was in these principles that Martin discovered his method for social reform. More than anything else, those two principles were the key to his achievements.

This book is about black Americans who served society through the excellence of their achievements. It forms a part of the rich history of black men and women in America—a history of stunning accomplishments in every field of human endeavor, from literature and art to science, industry, education, diplomacy, athletics, jurisprudence, even polar exploration.

Not all of the people in this history had the same ideals, but I think you will find something that all of them have in common. Like Martin Luther King, Jr., they all decided to become "drum majors" and serve humanity. In that principle—whether it was expressed in books, inventions, or song—they found something outside themselves to use as a goal and a guide. Something that showed them a way to serve others, instead of living only for themselves.

Reading the stories of these courageous men and women not only helps us discover the principles that we will use to guide our own lives, but it teaches us about our black heritage and about America itself. It is crucial for us to know the heroes and heroines of our history and to realize that the price we paid in our struggle for equality in America was dear. But we must also understand that we have gotten as far as we have partly because America's democratic system and ideals made it possible.

We still are struggling with racism and prejudice. But the great men and women in this series are a tribute to the spirit of our democratic ideals and the system in which they have flourished. And that makes their stories special, and worth knowing. ◆

1
AN END
AND
A BEGINNING

<hr>

IT WAS A perfect day for a hanging.

The autumn air was brisk as an eager crowd gathered at the edge of town. A hanging—especially the hanging of a slave—was a popular public spectacle in pre–Civil War Virginia, almost as exciting as a horse race. Fried chicken and biscuits were unpacked. Men took long pulls at the apple brandy that was Southampton County's most famous product. Older children ripped through the gathering crowd, while the little ones tugged at their mothers' skirts, wondering what all the excitement was about.

Suddenly, a mother stood and hoisted her baby to her shoulder. A father pulled his son from play and commanded him to pay attention. A wagon was approaching from the center of town, with armed men on horses riding in front and behind.

Nat Turner—a compact, muscular man about 30 years old—rode in the wagon, bound in chains. His broad, handsome African features were calm and composed; his brown eyes scanned the crowd without wavering. If he was looking for a friendly face, he was disappointed. All of the faces that he saw were white, and most were twisted with hatred. A few weeks before, when he was captured, the crowd had taunted him and spat at him, then beaten him with ropes and sticks. But on this day they were silent.

Turner's band of slave revolutionaries carved a trail of death in Virginia during their fierce bid for freedom in 1831. Turner met his own death with courage and dignity on the Southampton County "hanging tree," shown here as it appeared 60 years later.

Turner was imprisoned in the Southampton County Jail (shown here) after his capture. Calling himself a martyr for the cause of black freedom, the condemned man asked his accusers, "Was not Christ crucified?"

The wagon stopped. The jailer helped the prisoner down, then whispered in his ear as he led him toward the twisted old oak that served Southampton County as a hanging tree. The jailer had asked him if he had any last words that he wanted to say.

Turner shook his head. He had already had his say. In a long interview conducted in jail a few days before, he had told the story of the slave rebellion that he had led. That would be his statement for the world. "I am ready" was all he would now say.

Without flinching, Turner allowed a thick hemp rope to be put over his neck and the knot pulled snug. Ignoring the breathless crowd, he looked up for one last time at the autumn sky, towering with clouds. Then, without a flicker, he closed his great, dark eyes on the world.

The other end of the rope was thrown over a high limb. A ripple of excitement ran through the crowd as a few white men especially chosen for this honor spat on their hands and took hold of the rope. As they yanked the doomed man off his feet, the crowd gasped in anticipation.

Yet they were denied the spectacle that they had come to see. Turner died as he had lived: with the dignity and courage of a leader of men, and with a measure of mystery as well. Hoisted toward the Heaven that he firmly believed was preparing to receive him with honors, he hung perfectly still, as if already dead; he hung without a kick or a twitch, determined even in his last moments to deny his enemies the satisfaction of watching his torment.

It was Turner's last act, and it spooked the crowd. "Not a limb or a muscle was observed to move," an awed eyewitness reported.

Unnerved, disappointed, uneasy, the white people of southeastern Virginia went home—some to pitiful hardscrabble farms, some to vast plantations. Later in the evening, as their slaves watered and bedded the horses, they said their prayers, lit their lamps, and kissed their children good night, as they usually did.

But this night was also different. This night they locked their doors. They checked the pistols under their beds; they primed the shotguns leaning against the bedroom walls. They woke up at every moaning of the wind, every cracking branch, every cooing dove.

For Turner and the men who rode with him had put an end to the peaceful sleep of Virginia. By attacking slavery with the sword, they had shattered the complacency of the South. By organizing and leading the most successful slave revolt in American history, Turner had drowned in blood the absurd lie that blacks were happy as slaves and would submit forever to be the beasts of burden of whites.

Now everyone—both blacks and whites—knew that slavery would be stopped. It was only a matter of time. ❧

A preacher and mystic, Turner claimed that he had been chosen by God to bring about an end to the slave system. Although Turner was captured and hanged after his revolt, his bold act of defiance against the tyranny of slavery proved to be an inspiring symbol to other black rebels.

2
THE WORLD
OF
SLAVERY

N AT TURNER WAS born in Southampton County, Virginia, in 1800. According to legend, his mother was so determined not to subject him to a life of slavery that she tried to kill him as soon as he was born. She was tied to her bed and held away from him until she calmed down.

After that brief moment, however, Nat's mother lavished love and affection on him. To make him grow proud and independent, she continually told him of the greatness of his African heritage—even before he was old enough to understand her. If she could not keep him from being born into slavery, at least she could keep his young mind from being enslaved.

While Nat was still very young, his parents and grandmother searched his head and body for bumps and marks that were, in African religion and folklore, signs of prophecy. They then told him—and any others who would listen—that he was destined for great things. In his *Confessions*, written after the 1831 rebellion, Nat emphasized his parents' strong influence on his life by saying, "My father and mother strengthened me in this, my first impressions: that I was to be a Prophet."

While Nat was growing up in Virginia, he was surrounded by what was one of the cruelest systems of slavery ever established by mankind. The slave

Slave caravans transported yoked and bound captives from Africa's inland villages to ports on the coast. Turner's mother was among the tens of millions of Africans who were loaded onto ships and carried off to the Americas.

system in 19th-century America was built from an international slave-trade network that was founded in the 1520s. Men and women were stolen from their homes and farms in Africa, brought by Europeans to the colonies in the Americas, and condemned to perpetual servitude. For most, there was no hope, no reprieve from life as a slave.

The activities of this international slave-trade network remained legal until 1808, when the importation of slaves was outlawed by the governments of Great Britain and the United States. But because the legislation that abolished the importation of slaves was not widely enforced, slaves were still being imported from Africa while Nat was growing up in the early 1800s.

American slaveowners treated African-born slaves much more ruthlessly than they treated other people who worked as servants and laborers. Indentured servants who came to America from Europe worked for

An escaped slave named Margaret Garner stabbed to death two of her children to prevent them from being recaptured by slave-catchers. According to some accounts, Turner's mother similarly tried to kill him so that he would be spared from a life in slavery.

an agreed-upon period of time—five years, seven years—after which they were free. However, captured Africans remained as slaves until the day they died, and their children were regarded as slaves from the moment they were born. Even those few blacks who managed to buy their freedom or were released from slavery had no real freedom—neither in the British colonies nor after the colonies became the United States.

In the North as well as in the South, free blacks were denied almost all legal rights, including the right to vote, to live where they wanted, and to defend themselves or their property in court. Even when free blacks managed to scrape together a little land or some tools, or build or buy a house, their property might be taken away from them by whites. This was done through legal trickery or outright violence, in the same way that these blacks or their ancestors had been stolen from their homeland. Free blacks were sometimes even kidnapped and sold back into slavery.

In America, the slave system was based on a doctrine—still prevalent in parts of the world today—called white supremacy. The followers of this doctrine considered whites to be "more human" than other people. Consequently, whites had more rights to property, liberty, and happiness than any other people in the world. This doctrine conveniently allowed whites to enslave Africans and steal the land of the indigenous American people (whom the European settlers had mistakenly called Indians) with a clear—or almost clear—conscience.

Prejudice is as old as humanity itself and has been practiced by all peoples. However, white supremacy—holding that entire races are actually subhuman (somewhere between beasts and men)—was originally formulated in Europe, and it led to the cruelty of American slavery. The political and economic ef-

The slave trade was a profitable business for both northern shipping merchants and southern plantation owners. Strong, able-bodied field hands commanded huge prices, especially in the Deep South.

fects of this doctrine are still seen today in the depressed conditions under which blacks live in many parts of the world. The psychological effects are difficult to see and are even harder for whites to imagine. As David Walker, a free black abolitionist, wrote in his passionate *Appeal* of 1829:

> I call upon the professing Christians, I call upon the philanthropist, I call upon the very tyrant himself, to show me a page of history . . . which maintains that the Egyptians heaped the insupportable insult upon the children of Israel, by telling them they were not of the human family. Can the whites deny this charge? [Has not] Mr. [Thomas] Jefferson declared to the world, that we are inferior, both in the endowments of our bodies and our minds?

Composer of the Declaration of Independence, Thomas Jefferson supported the gradual abolition of slavery in the United States. Nonetheless, he owned many slaves and believed that blacks were inferior to whites. This page from his accounts book lists the slaves who worked at his Monticello estate.

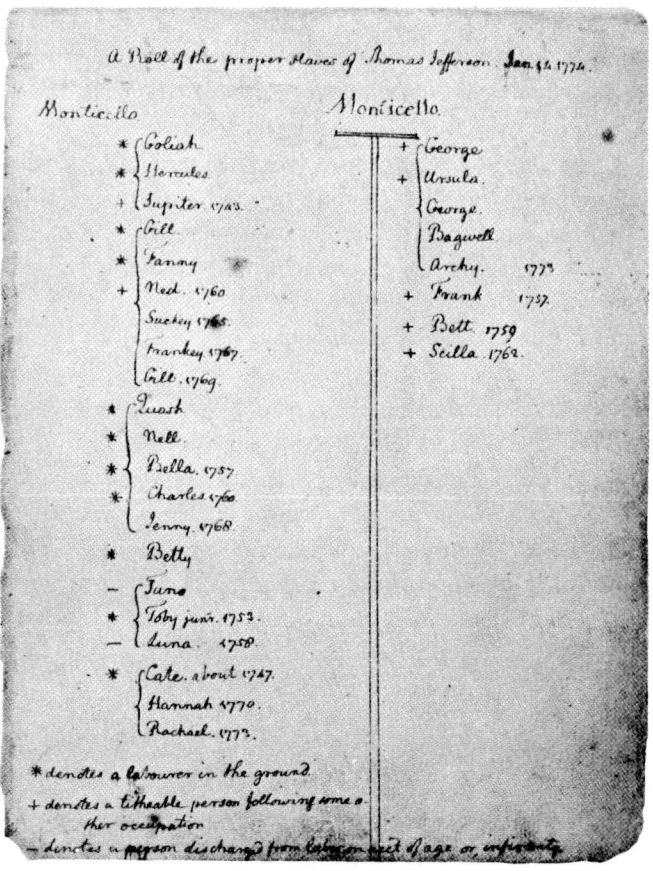

For more than 200 years—from the early 1600s until the 1860s—slaves in America produced rice, sugar, indigo, cotton, tobacco, coal, gold, lumber, and hemp worth billions of dollars. They cleared and fenced the land, built the barns and houses, plowed, harvested, and produced the wealth on which the growth of the United States was based. Yet neither they nor their descendants have ever been paid for this labor or compensated for the crime of being kidnapped from their native land.

This was the form of slavery that was practiced in the United States until it was abolished in 1865, after the Civil War, and it may have been even harsher than the form of slavery that was employed by either the ancient Egyptians or the ancient Romans. The

Slavery was a common practice in the Roman Empire and other civilizations of the ancient world. Wealthy people considered it a mark of distinction to own many house servants.

master of an American or Caribbean slave was usually a middle-class farmer who lived on credit, was always in debt, and had to push his slaves to produce more every year. Therefore, the slave's true master was the worldwide commodity system and its bottomless hunger for cotton and sugar.

Slaves in the South worked six or six and a half days a week, from sunup to sundown (from "can see" to "can't see"). The average slaveowner spent an estimated seven dollars a year per slave for food and about the same amount for clothing. Even at a time when seven dollars might equal a month's wages for a white farmworker, this amount was low enough to make slavery an extremely attractive system for slaveowners.

Historians sometimes write about how American slaves were rarely mistreated, how slaveowners were often kind, and how even those who were not kind were hardly stupid enough to mistreat their own valuable property any more than they would mistreat a horse or a piano. Yet people often mistreat animals, either through ignorance or malice. And while it is true that people rarely mistreat an object as valuable as a piano, a piano rarely rebels or resists.

Slaves often did resist, in big ways and small. They refused to work, or they worked slowly or "stupidly," sabotaging tools or crops. They ran away, joining the Indians or forming societies of their own, which were called Maroon societies, deep in the hills or the swamps. Traces of these societies exist today in Haiti, Guyana, and Jamaica. Their legacy can also be seen in the African coloring of the Florida Seminoles, who were a civilized people and took in runaways from the barbarism of slavery. There were even remnants of a Maroon society, Coe Ridge, in the hills of Kentucky until the 1940s.

However, most slaves—like most people—were not brave enough or lucky enough to run away and

Slave traders rarely showed any sympathy for their captives when they were auctioned off and their family ties were severed. Slaves were considered easier to train once they were completely cut off from their friends and relatives.

start a new life in the wilderness. For them, escape took the form of religion and storytelling—dreaming of another, better world—or else they put their hopes in their children, as so many people of all races do, even today.

It was into this strange, cruel world that an African teenager—said by legend to be a queen of the Sudan—was kidnapped in 1793. (Many of the stories that have been told about this young woman, who became Nat's mother, are really legends. Although not all legends are based on fact, they are still important because they tell us much about the hopes and dreams of the people who relate them.) Legend says that she was a queen, and perhaps she was: When wars took place between rival African states, many royal Africans were captured by their enemies and sold to European slave traders.

The young woman's owner called her Nancy, but this was not her real name (just as Nat was probably not the name that she gave to her son after he was born). Her real name was stolen from her—along with her language, her homeland, and her customs—because the slave system in America was threatened by slaves who remained bound to their original culture. Being given Christian names helped to complete their sense of alienation from their homeland and destroy their former identity.

It is said that Nat's mother was kidnapped from the ancient lands of the upper Nile and marched a thousand miles to the sea, chained in a long caravan with other captives, and then locked in the hold of a ship. There began the dreaded Middle Passage, a genocidal nightmare that rivals in horror the Holocaust that was carried out by Nazi Germany in the 1930s and the 1940s. As many as 5 to 10 million Africans died on the journey across the Atlantic Ocean, crammed into the airless holds of specially designed ships, where they could neither move nor sit nor stand. Only 18 inches of space were allotted for each man, woman, and child.

Once a day (when the weather permitted it), the slaves were taken on deck from the airless dungeon of the hold and were slopped like hogs with cornmeal from a barrel, splashed down with salt water, and then forced with whips back down into the darkness and their chains. Those who could make it to the side of the ship sometimes hurled themselves or their children over the side and into the ocean. Dead and sickly slaves were also thrown overboard by the crew. It is said that the shark population grew a thousand-fold during slavery and that they followed the ships in great gray schools under water. Folklore even says that it was the slave trade that introduced sharks to human flesh and made them man-eaters.

Those Africans who survived the Middle Passage were unloaded into dockside slave pens in Jamaica, Barbados, Georgia, and Virginia. They were cleaned up and fattened for a few weeks like cattle (and often branded with red-hot irons as well), then stripped naked, inspected from tooth to toe, and sold at auction. Babies were sold from their mothers' arms.

The cargo holds on slave ships were hellish prisons in which chained captives were kept penned close together and were given little food or water. Many slaves died or committed suicide during the torturous voyage across the Atlantic Ocean.

The African teenager who was to become Nat's mother arrived in Norfolk, Virginia, in 1797. She was angry, rebellious, and (although she probably tried not to show it) heartbroken because she was never to see her parents or loved ones again, never to see her home once more. If the legend is true and she was from the upper Nile, then she grew up in a land of ancient cities, awesome temples, and centers of learning and trade. What, then, did she think when she saw the slave ports of Tidewater Virginia, the crude cabins and log huts, the hogs running in the streets?

She was bought by a farmer named Benjamin Turner in 1799 and taken to his home in Southampton County. As crude as Norfolk was, one can only imagine what this teenager from the cradle of civilization thought of this region's scrub pine and swamp wilderness, where even the wealthiest planter lived in a board shack or a two-story "dogtrot" cabin. Southampton County in 1800 was a backwater. It took two days through the Great Dismal Swamp to get there from Norfolk; two days through the pine forests to get there from Richmond, the capital of Virginia; and a day to get there from the more settled areas of North Carolina, which were just to the south.

Benjamin Turner christened his newly acquired human property "Nancy," and her real name was lost to history. It is not known what her language was; it is said that she resisted speaking English for many years. Because she was rebellious, she was beaten often and severely.

At Benjamin Turner's farm, Nancy met "Old Bridget," who would soon become her mother-in-law. Although Bridget was only a generation away from Africa herself, it is doubtful that the two women spoke the same language; Africa, like Europe, is a continent of many tongues, and slaveowners were careful to separate slaves who spoke the same lan-

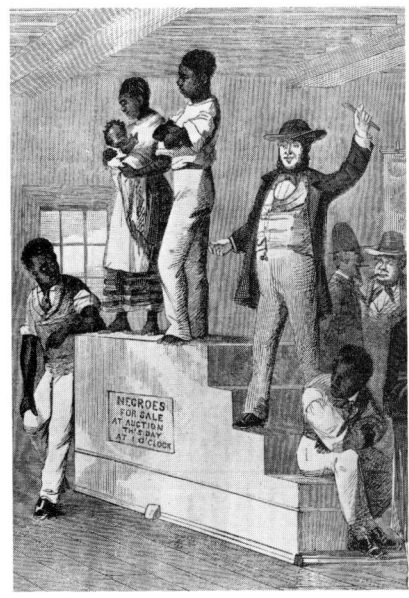

The agents of wealthy southern planters regularly attended slave auctions in search of promising workers. Occasional rebellions in the auction houses' slave pens were suppressed by the local militia.

The successful revolt against French rule carried out in the 1790s by slaves in Haiti was a tremendous inspiration to American slaves. Toussaint L'Ouverture (shown here) led the rebellion that gave birth to the first black nation in the Western hemisphere.

guage. Perhaps, in a final irony, the African teenager had to learn English so that she could converse with other Africans.

In her loneliness and desolation, Nancy was given—willingly or not, we will never know—to Bridget's son. Before the year 1799 was out, she was pregnant with a child who would become the property of Benjamin Turner, Esq., of Southampton County, Virginia.

Although the name of Nat's father has not been recorded, we know that he was only two generations removed from Africa himself, and we know from his later actions that he possessed a proud, rebellious spirit. We can only imagine that he loved his son and, like Nat's mother and grandmother, raised him with the belief that he was destined to be more than just a Virginia farmer's chattel.

Many changes and portents coincided with the start of the 19th century. To the south, on the French-ruled island of Santo Domingo, a fierce slave revolt was blazing into success. Haiti, the first black republic, was being wrested from the control of the French planters by the great black general Toussaint L'Ouverture. Slaveowners from Brazil to Virginia trembled in their boots at Toussaint's success. Slaves were rising up, arming themselves, killing their white oppressors, seizing the land, and setting up their own government. Is it any wonder that Thomas Jefferson and the Founding Fathers feared that their own slaves might do the same?

New laws were passed restricting free blacks. Garrisons were built and guns were stockpiled in every town, until every 10th person in Virginia was part of the armed militia. Slaves were forbidden to read or write, and on Sundays they were taught that slavery was blessed by God and sanctified in the Bible. Still, the slaves plotted rebellion. In southern Virginia, a group of slaves rose up and killed their overseers. They were hanged.

Then, in Richmond, also at the turn of the century, a slave named Gabriel Prosser organized the biggest slave revolt ever planned until then. Prosser even had a new flag made, saying that the Africans were going to take what the whites had taken from the British only a few years before: independence. Prosser's rebels intended to spare those few whites who had shown sympathy for the Africans and opposition to the slave system—mostly Quakers and some Methodists.

However, Prosser's rebellion was discovered. The leaders were captured, and the Americans showed their love of liberty by hanging all those Africans who had conspired to gain it.

During that same year, 500 miles to the north, John Brown was born—a white man who would go down in history as an enemy of slavery and a friend to the Africans.

It was in this portentous year of 1800 that Nat Turner was born.

The offices of slave dealers were common sights on the streets of southern cities. Many stores that sold farm equipment and livestock also held slave auctions.

3

A
SLAVE'S
DREAMS

WHAT WAS LIFE like for a slave child in the early 1800s? For years, the old folks remembered slavery days as "frock time" because women and children—boys as well as girls—went around in shapeless, baglike dresses or frocks. Nat did, too, until he was 12 years old.

Home for a typical slave family was a 16-foot square, windowless log hut with a dirt floor. Bed was a cornshuck-stuffed pallet in the corner or, for the fortunate child, perhaps a little loft. Breakfast was hoecakes (fried cornbread). Dinner was more cornbread, cabbage, black-eyed peas, and molasses. On Sundays or holidays there might be a little pigsfeet or fatback—leftovers from the whites at the "home house." Perhaps the head of the family had sneaked away during the week and snared a possum or caught some lazy catfish in one of the swampy ponds around Southampton County. As related in the "Uncle Remus" fables published by Joel Chandler Harris in the late 1800s, the slaves were clever at getting by and at coming up with little extra treats for their children.

A slave child was expected to start earning his or her keep at an early age. (This was true in industrial

Cotton was the chief crop grown on the farms in Virginia, where Turner was raised. Because the plant quickly exhausted the soil, the center of cotton production gradually moved to more recently settled areas in the Deep South and the West.

At an early age, slave children were put to work shelling peas and doing other light chores.

England, too, where free white children—at least, those of the poor—who were as young as eight were put to work in the mills and mines.) In Virginia, slave children were put to work around the yard and kitchen from about the age of 7 and were sent to the fields at the age of 12. Their childhood was brief.

Still, slave children managed to have some fun—at least when the white slaveowners were off to one of their many prayer meetings. Then there were children all over the place, bubbling over with joy and mischief. There was play—sometimes even with white children who were too young to understand that someday their playmates would be their property. It is said that one of the few whites who was spared by Nat's army during its bloody march across Southampton County was a man with whom Nat had played while he was a boy.

As in many agricultural or peasant societies where the women work in the fields with the men, the very young were watched over by the very old. Nat, like so many black children, grew up at the knees of the old folks—the ones with the stories, myths, and legends of their beloved African homeland still in their hearts. His early days were filled with stories about his heritage told to him not only by his mother but by others as well.

Nat's grandmother, Bridget, who had become a Christian, taught him about Christianity and probably showed him how to read as well. Nat was able to read at an early age, perhaps as young as five. This was very unusual in a country where most of the adult whites were illiterate.

There are several legends that are told about how Nat learned to read. He himself said that the alphabet "came to him" in a vision, the letters burning themselves into fallen leaves on the ground. He may have sincerely believed in such miracles, or he may have just been keeping a secret—that the old slaves taught the young ones some forbidden things.

Some historians maintain that Benjamin Turner's family taught Nat how to read. However, it was a criminal offense to teach a slave to read in those days, and although Benjamin Turner was a liberal Methodist, it is not likely that he was so liberal that he would attempt such a thing. Yet he did allow Nat to read once he discovered that Nat knew how; he even encouraged it—as long as Nat's reading was confined to the Bible.

Nat was also instructed in religion by his grandmother. He became a Christian, although it appears that he took less to the New Testament and its lessons of forgiveness, about which the slaveowners were always preaching to the slaves, and more to the stern righteousness, blood, and thunder of the Old Tes-

Although masters were forbidden from teaching their slaves how to read, some slaveowners organized Sunday school lessons. Turner was one of the few slaves who learned how to read, and he spent much time studying the words of the Old Testament's prophets and warriors.

tament prophets. Once he became a Christian, religion and freedom became tied together in his mind.

It is probable that Nat learned to respect African religion as well. One of the most trusted leaders of his rebellion was a "conjure man" trained in African folklore, medicines, rituals, and charms. From these religious teachings, Nat learned to be responsible and respectful to his elders.

Nat's father ran away from the Turner farm when Nat was only eight or nine. This must have been both the saddest and the happiest day of his young life: to know that your parent is gone, yet to know that he has flown to freedom. What a conflict of feeling the news of his father's escape must have produced in the young boy's heart! Although he missed his father, the example of his courage and daring was to stay with Nat all of his life.

One story has it that Nat's father escaped to the North; another has it that he made it back to Africa, to Liberia. However, another and more chilling story is still told around Southampton County. It says that Nat's father was betrayed after his escape and was sold to the turpentine plantations in Georgia, which few men survived. The story also says that when Nat later discovered that his father was not free but was

According to some historians, the farmhouse shown here belonged to Turner's first master, Benjamin Turner.

probably dead, it was the bitterest disappointment of his life.

Nat began to work all of the time when he was 12 years old, and the full bitterness of slavery was soon upon him. He worked from dawn to dusk plowing, hoeing, weeding, building fences, feeding animals, and gathering in crops. His owners were not rich, nor were they idle; they were farmers who sometimes even worked in the fields alongside their slaves. But as hard as the Turners worked, they were getting something in return for their efforts. They owned the land, and they owned the crops; the improvements as well as the profits were theirs.

As Nat toiled day and night for nothing, he watched as his own family—and his own people—sank deeper and deeper into ignorance and slavery. Because he knew how to read and knew about his heritage, he was better off than most other slaves. How many slaves knew nothing else but slavery? How many generations would it be before his people lost all memory of their former greatness, including their languages, their religions, and their history? How many gener-

While growing up, Turner sat by the fireplace in his cabin and listened to his grandmother and the other black elders tell stories about Africa, Jesus and his disciples, and slaves who escaped to freedom.

ations before all of their heroes were replaced by American heroes who were white? Before long, the slaves would become what their owners wanted them to be: not men but beasts of burden.

As Nat worked the sandy fields behind a plow, he thought deeply on these matters. One day, he claimed to have heard a voice that told him to seek "the Kingdom of Heaven." Perhaps this voice was as real to him as the voices in biblical times were to the prophets in the Old Testament; perhaps this voice was part of a religious parable made up by Nat so that white Christians would recognize that he was a human being just like themselves. In either case, the Kingdom of Heaven meant only one thing to a slave: freedom. However, Nat did not know at this point if the voice meant freedom just for himself, for his family and friends, or for his entire people.

When Nat was 20 years old, Virginia fell into an economic depression that lowered the price of land, farm commodities, and slaves. The price of cotton soon dropped dramatically, from 30 cents a pound to 10 cents a pound. The other main cash crops in Southampton County—apples, which were made into a crude brandy that was the most famous local specialty, and peanuts—also fell drastically in price.

Many of the farmers started to sell their land and move west and south, to Kentucky, Tennessee, Alabama, and Mississippi. Those farmers who managed to hold on to their land sometimes saw their children leave. Few new settlers moved in. The opening of the American frontier further helped to depopulate the Tidewater area—especially Southampton County, with its sandy, worn-out soil.

Because of the depression, slavery did not prove to be as profitable as it had once been in the part of Virginia where Nat lived. Many slaves were sold and transported out west and down south. Some bought their freedom with the money that they had managed

CAUTION!!

COLORED PEOPLE

OF BOSTON, ONE & ALL,

You are hereby respectfully CAUTIONED and advised, to avoid conversing with the

Watchmen and Police Officers of Boston,

For since the recent ORDER OF THE MAYOR & ALDERMEN, they are empowered to act as

KIDNAPPERS

AND

Slave Catchers,

And they have already been actually employed in KIDNAPPING, CATCHING, AND KEEPING SLAVES. Therefore, if you value your LIBERTY, and the *Welfare of the Fugitives* among you, Show them in every possible manner, as so many *HOUNDS* on the track of the most unfortunate of your race.

Keep a Sharp Look Out for KIDNAPPERS, and have TOP EYE open.

APRIL 24, 1851.

Pushed beyond his limit by a harsh slave overseer, Turner became a fugitive for 30 days before he decided to return to his master. Even if Turner had escaped to the North, he still would have faced the danger of being kidnapped by slavecatchers who roamed the streets of cities such as Boston.

to scrape together; not only could most slaveowners use the money, but when it came time for them to buy a new slave, one would not cost very much. Still other slaves were given their freedom. There was even talk of legally abolishing slavery.

In the early 1820s, there were about 1,700 free blacks living in the area around Jerusalem, Virginia. A few were independent farmers, but most worked for white farmers in return for a few dollars and a shack in which to live. Because their living conditions were not much removed from the conditions that they had endured when they had been slaves, the depression was harder on these free blacks than it was on the poorer white farmers.

One of the farmers who was hit hard by the depression was Benjamin Turner's son, Samuel. Forced to choose between selling his slaves or getting more profit out of them, Samuel hired an overseer to drive them harder. Among his slaves was Nat, whom Samuel had inherited from his father.

Nat promptly ran away. Patrols and hunting dogs were sent out to find him, and they combed the nearby swamps and woods. However, Nat was nowhere to be found.

Nat's fellow slaves prayed for him. After two weeks had passed, the slaveowners gave up their search. The slaves rejoiced in secret.

Yet they were all in for a surprise 30 days later, when Nat, who had eluded all of his pursuers, walked up to the front porch of his owner's house and gave himself up. The other slaves were furious with him. Why did he come back when he had gotten away clean? they wanted to know. Why did he turn himself in? These were good questions, but he did not give them an answer.

However, Nat later wrote in his *Confessions* that while he was in hiding, "the Spirit" had chastised him for having his wishes directed to the things of this world and not to the "Kingdom of Heaven." One way to interpret this statement is that he realized his destiny was not only to pursue his own freedom but the freedom of his people. He had bigger plans and a greater destiny than a simple escape. Thus, he chose to sacrifice his own freedom—just as he was to sacrifice his life—so that his people might have a chance to fight for their freedom.

Samuel Turner was so amazed to see a runaway slave return of his own free will that Nat went unpunished. He returned to his daily work—plotting, dreaming, biding his time. But now, at least, he was a young man who had a sense of what his mission was.

People often develop an interest in religion during hard times, and as the economic depression continued, many of Nat's fellow slaves turned to religion for comfort. In the rural areas of the South, camp meetings and religious revivals became very popular. Whites gathered in huge tent cities to take part in days of preaching, feasting, singing, and expressing their religious convictions. The staid, respectable English church (both the Episcopal and the Anglican church), with its polite hymns and solemn ceremonies, had become outdated. Americans wanted a fiery religion, with hell and damnation, shouting, moaning, speaking in tongues—and even the handling of snakes, and new churches began to spring up all over the South.

Many slaves found solace from their labors at loud, boisterous religious revival meetings. During one of these meetings, Turner received the first of his divine revelations, and he soon became convinced that it was his mission to lead his fellow slaves to the "Kingdom of Heaven," his phrase for freedom.

American slaveowners were fearful that invading British troops would be successful in inspiring wide-scale slave rebellions during the War of 1812. The uprisings never took place, and some blacks, such as these riflemen at the Battle of New Orleans, fought with the Americans.

The slaveowners wanted to share their Christian religion with the slaves—adapted to suit their own purposes, of course. They hired preachers to explain to the slaves that the slaves who were patient on earth would get their reward in Heaven. If a slave was whipped, worked to death, or separated from his family, he would only be that much happier in Heaven, where he would be united with his family at last.

The slaveowners hoped that the slaves would believe these explanations. Perhaps some slaves did believe them and looked forward to Heaven, figuring that the white slaveowners would all go to Hell for their sin of slavery. But for the most part, the slaves adapted the religion of their owners to meet their own ends. They studied the Old Testament, learned about Moses leading the Jews out of slavery in Egypt, and took a special interest in the stories about Judgment Day.

The slaves created their own churches, where they were able to gather among themselves away from the view of whites. In these churches, they not only practiced religion, for they were religious people, much like their owners, but also dreamed of freedom and discussed the many rumors and hopes that often swept through the countryside.

Most of these rumors concerned the British. The slaves were always hoping that the former rulers of the American colonies would go to war against the United States. Most slaves wanted the British to take control of America because the British often talked about abolishing slavery (they would ultimately do so in 1834).

During the War of 1812, the British had promised freedom to all of the slaves who were willing to rebel against their American masters. Although the opportunity never arose for the slaves to take advantage of this offer, they did not forget it. Consequently, the slaves in Virginia hoped that the British would again attempt to invade the United States, much as they had done toward the end of the War of 1812. When the possibility of a British invasion or some other way of fighting for freedom was discussed during a religious service, this talk was often couched in phrases from the Bible—such as "Day of Judgment," "crossing over Jordan," and "coming of the Jubilee"—just in case whites were listening or had sent spies.

One version of Judgment Day came to Nat and his family in the early 1820s, shortly after he was married. Not much is known about Nat's wife. Her slave name was Cherry, she lived on the Turner farm, and her husband trusted her with his most secret plans and papers. After his slave rebellion, she was beaten and tortured in an attempt to get her to reveal his plans and whereabouts. Although we cannot know for sure, it is probable that Nat never mentioned her in his *Confessions* because he wanted to spare her and their three children as much pain as possible.

In 1822, soon after Nat was married to Cherry, Samuel Turner died. His estate had to be divided up, and so his property had to be appraised. Nat, his wife, their children, his mother (as well as his grandmother—if she was still alive), and the other slaves on the Turner farm were lined up with the cows and tools and furniture. A few appraisers went down the line assigning a value to each lamp, each chair, each tool, and each human being (we can only imagine how this very common Virginia practice affected Nat).

Nat was valued at $400, the going price for a top field hand. Cherry was valued at only $40.

Then Nat and his family were treated as if they were nothing more than chickens or hogs. The family was separated. Nat's mother was told to stay with Samuel Turner's daughter on the Turner farm, while

Nat was sold to one farmer and his wife was sold to another.

Although this division of the family surely must have been painful, it could have been worse. Nat's new owner, Thomas Moore, was a neighbor of Giles Reese, who had become the owner of Nat's wife and his children. Also, Nat was lucky not to be sold either south or west, where strong black men were being shipped daily to work on cotton, hemp, and turpentine plantations to replace the laborers there who were literally being worked to death. Life in Southampton County for a slave was difficult, but it was not quite as harsh as life on those plantations.

Nevertheless, the daily toll of work—as well as the sorrow and the humiliation of slavery—was still hard on Nat and all of his fellow slaves. Yet he did not dwell on these topics. He saw himself as a man of destiny, and he not only dreamed of his own independence but of freedom for all of his people. ☙

A tragic and all-too-common fate for slave families was to be split up when a master died and his possessions were divided among his heirs. The death of Turner's master in 1822 resulted in Turner being separated from his wife, Cherry, and their children.

4

"PROPHET NAT"

WHILE NAT TURNER slaved for Thomas Moore, he devoted his life to religion—or so it seemed. In fact, he was planning his rebellion.

From 1825 to 1830, Turner served as a preacher because it gave him the ability (at least on Sundays) to travel around the neighborhood. He preached at different black churches: at the Turner chapel which his former master had built for his slaves, at the Barnes Church on the North Carolina line, and at churches in Jerusalem and nearby Greensville County.

Often fasting during the week, Turner studied and prayed when he was not working, keeping himself apart from others. "I studiously avoided mixing in society, and wrapt myself in mystery," he said. On Sundays, he used a resonant voice filled with poetry to share his visions with the other slaves. His visions were of conflict, struggle, and liberation.

"I saw white spirits and black spirits engaged in battle," he cried out from the pulpit. "And the sun was darkened—the thunder rolled in the heavens and the blood flowed in streams—and I heard a voice saying, 'Such is your luck, such are you called to see, and let it come rough or smooth, you must surely bear it.' "

Turner prepared his followers for an uprising by preaching to them that "the great day of judgment was at hand." Some of his impassioned sermons were delivered at the Southampton Methodist Church (shown here).

Turner told his congregation that while he was working in the fields, he saw figures drawn in blood on the leaves. He interpreted this vision for his eager listeners as "the Blood of the Savior, who was about to lay down the yoke he bore for the sins of men." According to Turner, his vision meant that "the great day of judgment was at hand."

Turner soon became the most sought after of all the black preachers for miles around. His fellow slaves knew what he meant by sin, they knew what he meant by judgment, and they knew what he meant by salvation. Freedom was on all of their minds.

A few whites also understood what Turner was talking about. Although Sally Moore, his new owner's wife, had known him for years and thought that he was docile, her brother Salathial warned her that Turner was "a negro of bad character" who was stirring up trouble. Other whites suspected him of being a "conjure man," or witch doctor, and wished that the Moores would keep him closer to home.

Yet the Moores believed that he was harmless. Turner was polite and respectful, if just a little bit reserved and distant. He did not drink, steal, or gamble. He knew everything that there was to know about farming, and he worked like a mule all week. So they let him enjoy his preaching.

The slaves held "Prophet Nat" in so much respect that it bordered on awe. His dedication and single-mindedness gave them confidence in his ability and judgment. Rural Virginians—both blacks and whites—were simple people in superstitious times, and they came to believe that Turner was a prophet who could cure ailing people just with his touch. Some people even thought that he was so magical that he could control the weather.

Turner's eloquence and conviction were so impressive that he convinced a white man, E. T. Brantley, to give up his wicked ways and converted the

man to Methodism. Brantley even asked Turner to baptize him—an unheard-of thing in such bigoted times. Although the Methodist church refused to approve the baptism of a white man by a black slave, the two men went ahead and made plans to perform the ceremony at a river.

One of the places at which Turner preached was the village of Cross Keys. While traveling to his Sunday services, he learned which slaves he could trust with his plans for a slave revolt.

Word of this event spread for miles around, and on the day of Brantley's baptism, a crowd gathered on the bank of the river and threatened Turner and Brantley. It must have taken much courage for both of them to defy the menacing racism of the hostile and curious mob, yet they proceeded with the ceremony. They waded into the river, and Turner baptized Brantley while the crowd hooted and jeered.

Turner worked hard as a preacher. One Sunday he was in Jerusalem, the next in Cross Keys, the next in Bethlehem Crossroads or Bellfield. During his travels, he always made sure to take a different route and visit with a different family until he knew every swamp,

In 1822, the revolutionary black leader Denmark Vesey plotted a massive rebellion among slaves in Charleston, South Carolina. The attempt failed when an informer betrayed the rebels shortly before the uprising was set to take place.

SECOND EDITION,

....

Negro Plot.

—

AN ACCOUNT

OF THE LATE

INTENDED INSURRECTION

AMONG

A PORTION OF THE BLACKS

OF THE

City of Charleston, South Carolina.

Published by the Authority of the Corporation of Charleston.

....

BOSTON:

PRINTED AND PUBLISHED BY JOSEPH W. INGRAHAM,

1822.

every thicket, every forest, every dirt road, path, barn, shack, shed, and house within 30 miles. He was nothing if not thorough.

In between preaching, planning, and working, Turner spent as much time as possible with his wife and children at the Reese farm. He got to know everybody in the area, both blacks and whites. He knew which whites were mean to their slaves and which ones were not. He knew which blacks were bold and which ones were not. And he knew who could be trusted and who was a betrayer, eager to curry favor with his master.

This last piece of information was particularly important because the two largest slave rebellions until that time had both been betrayed by other blacks. Gabriel Prosser's rebellion in Richmond had been doublecrossed by one of his own people, and in 1822, even more heartbreaking news for rebellion-minded slaves had come from Charleston, South Carolina. An immense slave uprising led by a free black named Denmark Vesey had been betrayed to the whites and had failed.

Vesey was not unlike Turner in that he learned how to read and write and eventually devoted his life to the liberation of his people. He struggled to convince them to stop taking the insults of the slaveowners and to consider themselves as men. The next step after convincing them of this was to organize a rebellion.

Vesey and his recruits made their plans in strict secrecy. At the stroke of midnight, six organized battle units were to seize the town, seal off the major roads, and kill the plantation owners in their houses. Then they would either seize Charleston or, if that seemed impossible, commandeer a ship in the harbor and sail for the black republic of Haiti. Vesey's chief lieutenant, an African "conjure man" named Gullah (Angola) Jack, gave all of the recruits a crab claw as

The revolt of African captives on the Spanish vessel Armistad was the most famous of the slave rebellions that took place on board ships in the 19th century. The rebels won their freedom and were eventually allowed to return to Africa.

a good-luck token and a sign that the ancient African gods were watching over them.

The conspiracy was huge. Vesey had not only organized the free blacks in the town but also the slaves on the surrounding plantations, taking hundreds into his confidence. That was his mistake. Some of the house servants were loyal to their masters and gave away Vesey's plans.

Vesey was arrested along with 70 others, including a few whites who were helping because they also wanted to do away with the slave system. He and 35 others were hanged, while 37 more blacks were sent to a penal colony—and certain death—in the Caribbean. Vesey and his men went to their deaths with their heads held high, never revealing any of the details of their conspiracy.

When the rebellion was over, the slaveowners in South Carolina breathed easier. However, on Christmas Eve in 1825 and every night thereafter for six months, buildings in Charleston were torched, once again creating terror among the town's white residents.

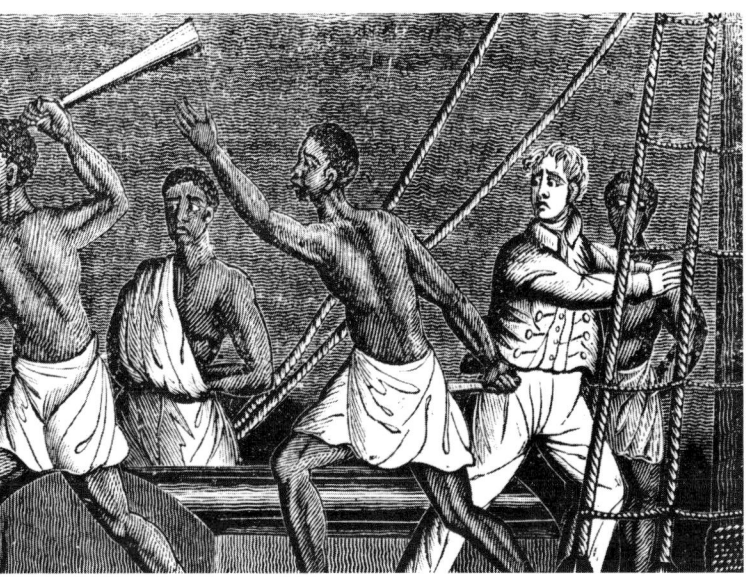

News traveled swiftly among the slaves throughout the country, so it is very likely that Turner was familiar with Vesey's rebellion in Charleston and became determined to emulate his courage while avoiding his errors. Consequently, Turner moved very slowly and deliberately, and his efforts paid off in the end, for his slave rebellion was not only the biggest and bloodiest in American history, but it was the most unexpected. Very few whites suspected what was brewing around them. As a white survivor in the area later said, "Not one note of preparation was heard to warn the devoted inhabitants of woe and death."

In addition to the slaves who knew and trusted Turner in the late 1820s, there were nearly 1,750 free blacks living in Southampton County. Many were servants, farm laborers, and sharecroppers, but some were independent small farmers and craftsmen, much like the dissatisfied free blacks who plotted with Vesey. One of Turner's most trusted followers was Billy Artis, a free black who owned a 14-acre farm yet was married to a slave woman. He knew that without freedom for all of his people, his own individual freedom was a

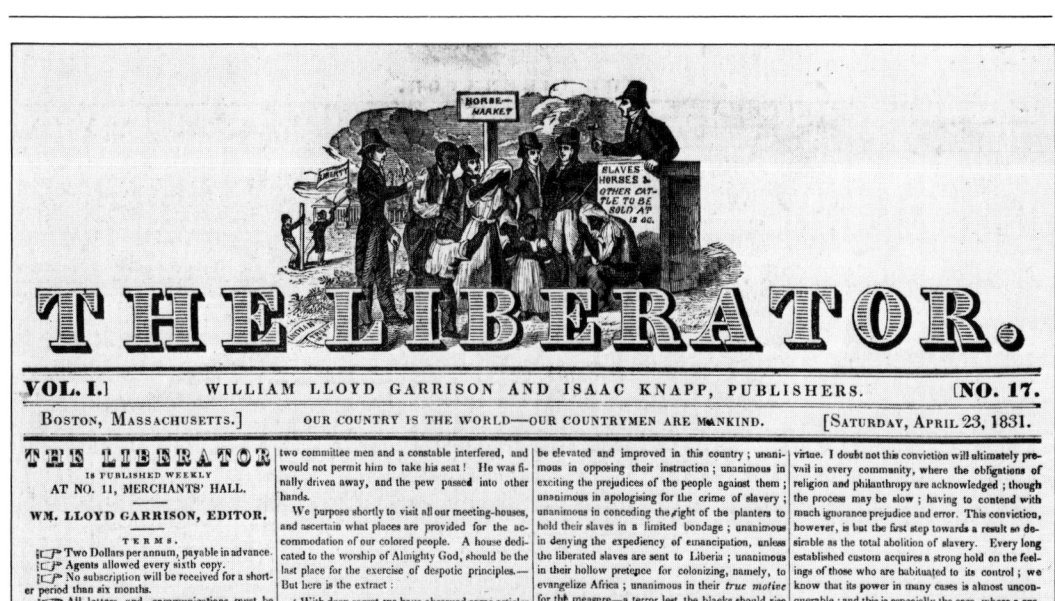

The most militant of the white abolitionist leaders during the 1830s was William Lloyd Garrison, who began publishing his highly influential newspaper, the Liberator, *eight months before Turner's rebellion. Slaveowners were infuriated with Garrison and accused him of trying to incite black uprisings in the South.*

charade. Consequently, he decided to join Turner's rebellion.

While Turner was making his plans and gathering his forces, the same stirrings of freedom were being felt around the country and in other parts of the world. The abolitionist movement, which demanded that human slavery be outlawed, was beginning to grow into a national movement, although it would not reach its full strength until after 1830. The first and the most radical of the abolitionists were black, but many whites—especially in the North—joined the movement as time went on.

Among the better-known white abolitionists who were believers in human rights and equality were

William Lloyd Garrison, who edited *The Liberator*, one of the nation's most popular antislavery newspapers, and John Brown, who ultimately gave his life while fighting slavery. Almost 30 years after Turner led his rebellion, Brown led an armed group of black and white abolitionists who attempted to capture the federal arsenal at Harpers Ferry, Virginia.

There were many different types of abolitionists. Some were against slavery on moral grounds, while others were against it for political reasons. Some—like the armed bands that were organized to defend runaway slaves in the northern cities—believed in taking action against slavery; in many cases, they opened fire on southern slavecatchers and sent them packing. Other abolitionists only believed in "moral persuasion" and never broke the law or threatened violence against the slaveowners. Some combined both methods—such as the Quakers, who would hide escaped slaves but would refuse to fight.

Some whites were against slavery without advocating freedom for blacks or equal rights. Many of these whites simply thought it best to ship all of the blacks in America back to Africa. They hated slavery only because they saw that it was ultimately dangerous to the whites. Others felt as well that they did not want free blacks living in "their" America.

The most militant abolitionists, of course, were the slaves themselves. They took part in slave revolts in Martinique, Cuba, and Jamaica as well as in the United States. In the fall of 1826, a group of slaves that was being taken from Maryland to Georgia hijacked the slave ship *Decatur*, killed two crew members, and sailed for Haiti. They were eventually captured, but when the ship was brought into New York City's harbor, all but one of the captives escaped to freedom. In Alabama, fugitive slaves who built a fort in the swamps were finally subdued, but not be-

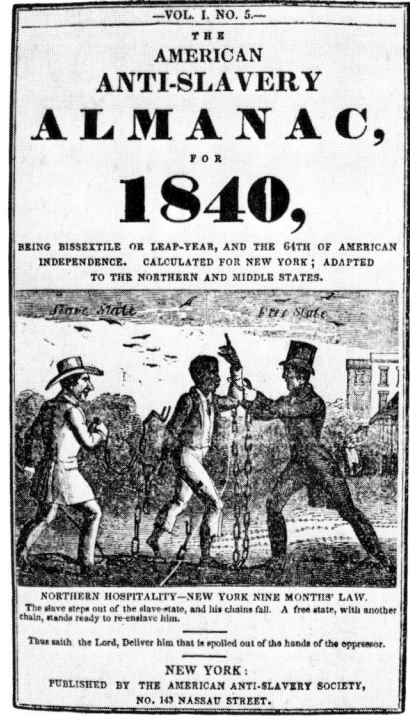

The American Anti-Slavery Almanac *and other publications distributed by the northern abolitionist societies were banned in the South, but some contraband copies were smuggled in on ships.*

fore the slaves, according to one report, had "fought like Spartans . . . and not one gave an inch of ground."

Echoing this militancy, the antislavery movement grew. Abolitionists spoke on the streets and in the churches in such northern cities as Boston, Massachusetts, and Philadelphia, Pennsylvania. However, abolitionists did very little campaigning against slavery in the South, where relatively few people were literate. Only people who knew how to read could be influenced by the abolitionists' published arguments. That is a major reason why slaves were not allowed to learn how to read and why it was a crime to teach reading to a slave. It is also why Turner's literacy was such an important aspect of his contribution to his people's struggle for freedom.

The governments of slave states such as Virginia did all that they could to keep abolitionist propaganda out of their states. The piece of literature that government officials hated the most—and the one that was perhaps an inspiration to Turner and other rebels around the country—was a book written by a free black abolitionist named David Walker. Originally published in Boston in 1829, *David Walker's Appeal to the Colored Citizens of the World, But in Particular, and Very Expressly, to Those of The United States of America* remains one of the most devastating, eloquent indictments of American slavery ever written.

In his *Appeal*, Walker called American slavery the cruelest and most hypocritical system that has ever existed because it dehumanizes its victims while flourishing in a so-called democracy. In particular, he had nothing but scorn for the white abolitionists who wanted to rid the country of blacks. "America is our country more than it is the whites," he said. "We have enriched it with our blood and tears."

Circulated chiefly by the author himself, Walker's *Appeal* was a direct call to his enslaved brethren in the South to strike boldly at their oppressors:

WALKER'S

APPEAL,

IN FOUR ARTICLES,

TOGETHER WITH

A PREAMBLE,

TO THE

COLORED CITIZENS OF THE WORLD,

BUT IN PARTICULAR, AND VERY EXPRESSLY TO THOSE OF THE

UNITED STATES OF AMERICA.

Written in B ston, in the State of Massachusetts, Sept. 28, 1829.

SECOND EDITION, WITH CORRECTIONS, &c.

BY DAVID WALKER.

1830.

Black abolitionist David Walker's antislavery pamphlet aroused a storm of controversy throughout America when it was published in 1829. His Appeal urged slaves to fight back against their oppressors and asked them, "Had you not rather be killed than be a slave to a tyrant?"

Should the lives of such creatures be spared? . . . Are they not the Lord's enemies? Ought they not to be destroyed? . . . If you commence, make sure work— do not trifle, for they will not trifle with you—they want us for their slaves, and think nothing of murdering us in order to subject us to that wretched condition— therefore, if there is an attempt made by us, kill or be killed.

During the 1820s, the Underground Railroad helped thousands of runaway slaves travel "freedom's road" to areas of relative safety in the North. However, for every refugee who escaped, many more were killed or recaptured.

This was strong talk by a skilled writer—indeed, one of the best of his day—and Walker's *Appeal* immediately sent shock waves of panic through the South. His book was promptly banned everywhere that slavery existed, and a price was put on his head. Walker died under mysterious circumstances only a year after his *Appeal* was published. It has been suspected that he was poisoned by friends of slavery in the North.

Walker's words soon proved to be a chilling foreshadowing of the fate of the slaveowners, who were killed by Turner and his men within two years of the publication of the *Appeal*. "They keep us miserable now," he said of the slaveowners, "and call us their property, but some of them will have enough of us by and by—their stomachs will run over with us; they want us for their slaves, and shall have us to their fill."

The words that so alarmed the slaveowners must have sounded like the pealing of a liberty bell to Turner. Although he never mentions Walker's book in his *Confessions*, the whites of Virginia never doubted that the hated *Appeal* contributed to Turner's rebellion. He might well have heard of it through word of mouth.

Yet Walker's words did not reach Virginia until almost the end of the 1820s, and Turner's course had been set several years before. During most of the years from 1825 to 1830, he was biding his time, waiting, trusting in the God in whom he sincerely believed: the God of judgment and salvation, who had promised him a sign.

Meanwhile, Turner continued his planning, getting to know the people, both black and white. Slowly and patiently, he was gathering his forces together, as a storm cloud gathers its energy for the lightning stroke that will illuminate both heaven and earth in one tremendous flash. ☙

5

"OURS IS
A FIGHT
FOR FREEDOM"

THE FIRST SIGN came on May 12, 1828. There was, as Turner later said, a "great noise" in the heavens. He stated that after this noise, "the Spirit instantly appeared to me and said the Serpent was loosened, and Christ had laid down the yoke he had borne for the sins of men, and that I should take it on and fight against the Serpent, for the time was fast approaching when the first should be last and the last should be first."

Other signs in the heavens would show Turner when to begin. He understood that after seeing these signs, "I should arise and prepare myself, and slay my enemies with their own weapons."

However, until these signs arrived, Turner kept this prophecy to himself. He prepared himself but withheld the details of his plans from even his closest and most trusted followers. He only slipped once, when he remarked to his owner, Thomas Moore, that the slaves would surely be free "one day or other." After hearing Turner say this, Moore beat him with a whip.

Later that same year, Moore died and Turner became the property of Moore's nine-year-old son, Putnam. Moore's widow, Sally, soon married Joseph Travis, a carriage maker from Jerusalem, who moved his business to the country and took up supervision of the farm, including all 17 slaves.

Entitled "Southern Industry," this engraving depicts a typical slave. Among the slaves and freedmen in Southampton County who were willing to sacrifice their lives for the chance to win their liberty with Turner were Hark Travis, Nelson Williams, Sam Francis, Henry Porter, Billy Artis, and Barry Newsome.

Turner continued working, keeping his mouth shut and his eyes open. He was looking for another sign. It came in February 1831, when a major eclipse of the sun took place. The eclipse was so striking and so unexpected that superstitious people of all races thought that the end of the world was at hand.

Turner, on the other hand, took this spectacular heavenly event as the sign he had been waiting for, and began to pull his plan together. He told his trusted inner circle to prepare their weapons, inform their contacts, and wait. The time to strike was approaching.

Turner had chosen for his inner circle about 20 people, all of whom he trusted completely. He chose so wisely and kept his secrets so well that today we only know the names of about seven or eight of his confidants. His wife, Cherry, was one. She was entrusted with maps written with pokeberry ink (made from a purple berry that grows wild in the South), lists in code, and strange ciphers that have never been deciphered to this day.

Hark, a slave at the Travis farm, was Turner's second in command. The name "Hark" was short for Hercules and was given to Turner's second because he was a giant. He looked like a "black Apollo," according to the whites.

Nelson Williams lived on the Williams farm, four miles southwest of Jerusalem. He was said to have special privileges—as Turner did—and was allowed to come and go as he pleased. A respected leader of the slaves, he was rumored by both blacks and whites to be a conjurer with supernatural powers.

Henry Porter and Sam Francis were said to be a bit more ordinary. Both lived near Turner and were reliable and well liked, although they apparently were not leaders. Henry Porter was one of 30 slaves on a good-sized plantation, and his task was to recruit for Turner among his fellow slaves. Sam Francis was owned

by Sally Travis's brother, so he had freedom of movement between the two farms.

Among the others whom Turner held in confidence were Billy Artis and Barry Newsome, two free black men in the neighborhood. Billy Artis was an independent farmer and—as he would ultimately show—a noble warrior. Not much is known about Barry Newsome except that Turner trusted him, which is a high enough recommendation for any man.

Turner began to meet and conspire in secret with these confederates. They compiled a list of 18 or 20 other trustworthy blacks. Most likely, they planned their route, tallying up the number of slaves and firearms, horses and mules on each plantation and farm between the Travis place and Jerusalem. This was the information Turner had spent years in gathering.

They set their target date for July 4, 1831, because it was a holiday. On that date, work was usually light and slaves were allowed to move around, while the whites were at ease or even drunk. Also, one suspects,

An eclipse of the sun in February 1831 was taken by Turner to be a sign from Heaven that he should begin plotting his rebellion. Gathering a group of trusted confederates, he told them of his visions of a world in which "the thunder rolled in the heavens, and blood flowed in streams."

Commonly subjected to brutal whippings and even maimings, some slaves were too terrified of their masters to join the front ranks of a liberation army. Turner hoped that once he established control of Southampton County, most of the area's slaves would rally to his cause.

the date was chosen for its ironic significance. As the black abolitionist and former slave Frederick Douglass was to point out later to the whites, "This is your holiday, not mine. You rejoice; we mourn."

Further arrangements were made. However, the rebels were frustrated in their efforts when Turner became sick as the fateful day drew near, and the rebellion was temporarily postponed. So many plans had been considered and rejected that, as he later explained, "it affected my mind." Perhaps his sickness was due to nervousness, fear, dread, anticipation; after all, the destiny for which he had been preparing for at least 10 years—and probably more—was about to come to pass.

Where did these doubts and fears come from? Surely Turner knew that he was taking on a well-armed and vicious enemy. Every slave uprising so far had failed and had been followed by mass hangings of black slaves. He was vastly outnumbered; even though Southampton County contained as many blacks as whites at that time, none of the blacks were armed and not all were willing to fight. They were psychologically unprepared, too. Many slaves believed that the whites were unbeatable, and Turner knew that it would take a few successes before significant numbers joined his rebellion.

The whites, on the other hand, were well prepared, even if they could be caught off guard. Slaveowners in Virginia told the world that their slaves were docile and content, but the slaveowners knew better than to believe their own propaganda. The Virginia militia was 10,000 strong, and there were numerous other volunteer military organizations. There were also the county patrols—the "paddy rollers" or "redlighters"—who rode the sandy roads with pitch pine torches pursuing runaways. Behind all this was the awesome power of the federal government, garrisoned at Fort Monroe in Norfolk.

To battle against this manpower, the slaves—disorganized, scattered, and unarmed—had only their desperation and desire for freedom. Also working against them was the knowledge that many revolts had been tried but none had succeeded. The always-present threat of betrayal and the need for secrecy meant that Turner's forces had to be kept extremely small—at least at the beginning, until after the first few blows had been struck.

All of these thoughts and more must have been going through Turner's mind, testing his determination, as the Fourth of July approached. We know from his *Confessions* that he was prepared to undergo the horrors of war and that he did not expect to survive ("Let it come rough or smooth, you must surely bear it," his vision had warned him). We also know that for several years he had sacrificed the meager family life that slavery allowed him, choosing instead to travel on his rare days of rest so that he could gather his forces and learn about the roads and the people around him.

A 13-year-old slave in Maryland at the time of the Southampton revolt, Frederick Douglass was deeply inspired by Turner's act of defiance. When Douglass later became an abolitionist newspaper editor in the North, he wrote, "We hold [slavery] to be a system of lawless violence; that it never was lawful and never can be made so."

Turner was certainly not a stonehearted fanatic. He was motivated by love—for his God, his family, and his suffering fellow blacks. He must have known even when he was playing with his two sons and his daughter (the children who were separated from him by slavery) that by fighting for their freedom, he would probably be igniting a holocaust around them— one that might consume them all. It is also likely that Turner's conscience was filled with David Walker's words: "I therefore ask the whole American people, had I not rather die, or be put to death, than to be a slave to any tyrant, who take not only my own, but my wife and children's lives by inches?"

Turner's hesitation in starting the rebellion is understandable. Yet his resolve was unshaken. Although July 4 came and went, the next and final sign came soon after.

On Saturday, August 13, there was such a strange darkness in the atmosphere that one could look directly at the sun. It seemed to shimmer and change colors—from green to blue to white. The phenomenon was visible along the entire eastern seaboard of the United States, and it made people fearful.

Then there was an even more awesome occurrence: A black spot appeared on the sun, passing slowly across its fiery surface. At this sign, Turner put his hesitations aside and called together his "chosen four": Hark Travis, Nelson Williams, Henry Porter, and Sam Francis.

"Just as the black spot passed over the sun," Turner told them, "so shall the blacks pass over the earth."

The word went out—cautiously but swiftly—to the other waiting slaves. The storm clouds began to gather. Only a few incidents, which were revealed later in the trials of the insurgents, gave any indication that something unusual was about to happen.

On the following Sunday morning, some whites who were passing a slave church near the boundary

$100 REWARD!

RANAWAY

From the undersigned, living on Current River, about twelve miles above Doniphan, in Ripley County, Mo., on 2nd of March, 1860, **A NE GRO MAN,** about 30 years old, weighs about 160 pounds; high forehead, with a scar on it; had on brown pants and coat very much worn, and an old black wool hat; shoes size No. 11.

line between Virginia and North Carolina noticed that the slaves were more "disorderly" than usual. They were rapturously listening to a thunderous "hell and damnation" sermon. The preacher was Nat Turner.

On Monday, August 15, a slave girl overheard several slaves in a cabin on the Solomon Parker farm. She noticed that two of them were visitors from neighboring Sussex County. In low tones, they said, "If the black people come this way, we will join and kill the white people." One of the slaves said that he had had his ears cut off by his master and vowed that the man would find his own cropped in return before the year was out.

On Thursday, a slave named Isham told another slave, "General Nat is going to rise and murder all the whites." Blacks must join the revolt, Isham said, or the whites would win and then kill all of the slaves.

Later reports show that in Virginia and in North Carolina—in Southampton and in the neighboring counties—many of the slaves knew that something

Turner's rebels knew that the price of failure would be heavy. Those who escaped from vengeful companies of white militia would be hounded by notices advertising large rewards for the recapture of fugitives.

Because Turner and his fellow rebels kept their plans so well guarded, the whites in Southampton County had no inkling that a slave revolt was about to occur. The house shown here belonged to the county sheriff Clements Rochelle.

was about to happen. However, they were not (or claimed they were not) exactly sure of what it was or when it would take place.

When the rebels were put on trial later on, as a reign of white terror ravaged the countryside, many blacks were eager to show their loyalty to the whites by denouncing Turner. It must be noted, though, that before the rebellion took place, not a word was heard. Turner had planned well.

August seemed to be a good month for Turner and his men to strike. Because it was a time when the crops had already been planted and the harvest had not yet begun, everyone's workload was relatively light. And Sunday was the lightest workday of all. The slaves had time for hunting and fishing while the whites went to church and then drank apple brandy and visited neighbors and relatives for the rest of the day.

On the evening of Saturday, August 20, 1831, Turner laid down his farm tools for the last time. He told Hark to prepare a dinner for Sunday at Cabin Pond, in the woods at the back of the Travis place, and to bring together the "chosen four."

Perhaps Turner visited his family at the Reese farm on Sunday morning, secretly giving his children a final kiss and having a tearful farewell with his wife. He took his time joining his men, not wanting to seem too familiar to them. He had studied why the French emperor Napoleon and the liberator Toussaint L'Ouverture were successful leaders, and he knew that the authority of a leader was increased by a little mystery and aloofness.

On Sunday afternoon, at about three o'clock, Turner joined his men at Cabin Pond. He found them sitting around a fire, roasting a pig and sharing some apple brandy. There were Hark Travis and Nelson Williams, Henry Porter and Sam Francis, and two new recruits: Jack and Will, a slave owned by Nathaniel Francis. Turner knew Jack, but he was unsure of Will and challenged him: "How came you here?"

Will answered, "My life is worth no more than the others, and my liberty is as dear to me."

"Do you think to obtain it?"

"I will, or lose my life."

Satisfied with this answer, Turner welcomed him.

The men sat around the fire and made their final plans. They decided to strike that very night. They would begin with Turner's masters, the Travis family, relying on sheer terror and speed to give them the initial advantage.

According to black folklore, Turner gave a final speech to his men in which he laid out their strategy and goals. He said, "Remember, we do not go forth for the sake of blood and carnage; but it is necessary that, in the commencement of this revolution, all the whites we meet should die, until we have an army strong enough to carry out the war on a Christian basis. Remember that ours is not a war for robbery, nor to satisfy our passions; it is a struggle for freedom."

Turner warned them to "spare neither age nor sex." Then they all stood, doused the fire, picked up their weapons—at that point only hatchets and knives—and set out across the fields and through the woods on the bloody journey that would carry them into history. ❧

"GENERAL NAT"

AT TWO O'CLOCK in the morning on Monday, August 22, 1831, Turner and his band of men stood in the yard of the Travis house. They were joined by two other slaves, Austin and a teenager named Moses. They approached the house. Hark wanted to break through the door with his axe, but Turner held him back, worried that the noise might wake the nearest neighbor, whose house was less than a half mile away. The night was deep and silent, and Turner wanted to preserve the element of surprise as long as possible.

Hark fetched a ladder and placed it against the side of the house. Turner waved him and the other men aside and climbed it alone. It was important to him that he actually lead the way, at least at the beginning.

After a few breathless moments, when the only sounds in the yard were the crickets and the frogs in the distant ponds, the downstairs door was unbarred with a muffled thud and Turner's whisper came from the darkness inside: "The work is now open to you." The rebels poured into the house as silently as shadows, their knives and axes gleaming in the moonlight.

Turner began his revolt early in the morning of August 22, 1831. The rebels vowed that they would spare no white man, woman, or child on their march to the nearby town of Jerusalem.

With Will close behind him, Turner led the way to the upstairs bedroom, where Joseph Travis and his wife were sleeping. As the General, the Prophet, the leader of the rebellion, Turner knew that he must strike the first blow and draw first blood. He struck with a blunt sword, and the master of Travis farm screamed bloody murder. Will moved in from behind and finished off Travis and his wife before they were fully awake.

Downstairs, the other men began to kill the rest of the whites in the house—one of them being 12-year-old Putnam, Turner's legal master. Soon all in the house were dead but an infant, momentarily forgotten in its cradle. Remembering Turner's instruction to "spare neither age nor sex," Henry Porter and Will returned upstairs and killed the child.

After the screams and blows, there was silence once again. But now there was also the smell of blood,

The rebels carried out their grisly work with ruthless efficiency, making sure that they left no survivors who could spread an alarm. This old woodcut illustration depicts the massacre of the Travis family and the fight with John Barrow.

dark and sticky, on the plank floor. Jack was sick to his stomach in the yard. Moses grew afraid, but he followed the others anyway. Both were learning that freedom can carry a great and awful price.

From the Travis house, they took four rifles, several old muskets, and some gunpowder. Leading his men to the barn, Turner armed them and drilled them with the weapons, marching them up and down to impress on them the fact that they were not outlaws or bandits but soldiers—soldiers of their people.

The next farm that they reached belonged to Sally Travis's brother, Salathial. It was he who had warned her that Turner was not just an innocent and carefree preacher, and tonight his fears were to be fully justified. Henry Porter and Will knocked on the door, telling the man that they had a letter for him. When he opened the door, he was pulled outside into the yard and was cut down.

In perfect silence and order, the rebels marched on, toward the town of Jerusalem more than 10 miles away. Turner had ordered that no firearms were to be used as of yet. Either at Salathial Francis's or along the way, he obtained a light sword, which he carried as a symbol of his command.

At the next darkened farmhouse, an old woman and her son were killed. As Turner later said in his *Confessions*, the son awoke during the rebels' attack, "but it was only to sleep the sleep of death, he had only time to say, 'who is that?' and he was no more."

Another house was passed by because its owner saw them coming and barricaded himself inside. "Here I am, boys!" he dared them. "I will not go from my home to be killed." Turner decided that the house was not worth attacking; the noise of the battle would arouse the neighbors. Instead, the rebels raced on toward town, picking up more slaves at every stop.

The first shots were fired near dawn, when it was no longer possible to catch people asleep in their beds. Ironically, these shots came at the old Turner place, where the slave revolt leader had lived for 10 years. The farm was now a plantation with 18 slaves. The overseer was taken by surprise at the cider press and was shot lest he warn the people in the house.

However, the shot proved to be enough of a warning. Widow Turner and a visiting neighbor tried to lock themselves inside the kitchen, but their efforts were of no use. The door was bashed down with an axe and both women were killed.

By the time that daylight came and the other white slaveowners were beginning to wake up, the rebels had become a full company of 15 armed men, 9 of them mounted. Turner split up his forces, sending 6 men to one farm and 9 to another. At each farm, what he later called "the work of death" was gruesome. However, the rebellion had not yet turned into a full-fledged fight. The rebels still had the advantages of speed and surprise.

Turner discovered that his sword was too dull for fighting, but he continued to carry it anyway. There were plenty of fighters now, and they were as eager as he and far more skilled.

At every homestead, all of the whites were killed without exception and all of the slaves who were willing to join the fight were recruited. Those who had no stomach for the rebellion were warned not to betray or interfere with it in any way. Then each house was searched for firearms, ammunition, food, clothing, and money. Horses and mules were saddled and taken. There was no petty individual looting, and in no instance were individuals humiliated or tortured, nor were women molested or raped.

The only lapse in the discipline of Turner's army was brought about by the apple brandy that was found in every Southampton home. Even though Turner was never known to drink, he initially permitted his men to imbibe at every stop. In doing so, he allowed a thief into the army's ranks—one that would eventually steal the men's resolve. However, this problem was not to surface until later on.

Francis. Travis. Whitehead. Bryant. Newsome. The homesteads fell one by one as the rebels rode toward Jerusalem, destroying the slaveowners farm by

While ransacking the farms of their masters, Turner's soldiers collected muskets that they would need to fight against well-armed militia companies. Most of the guns that they found were in poor condition.

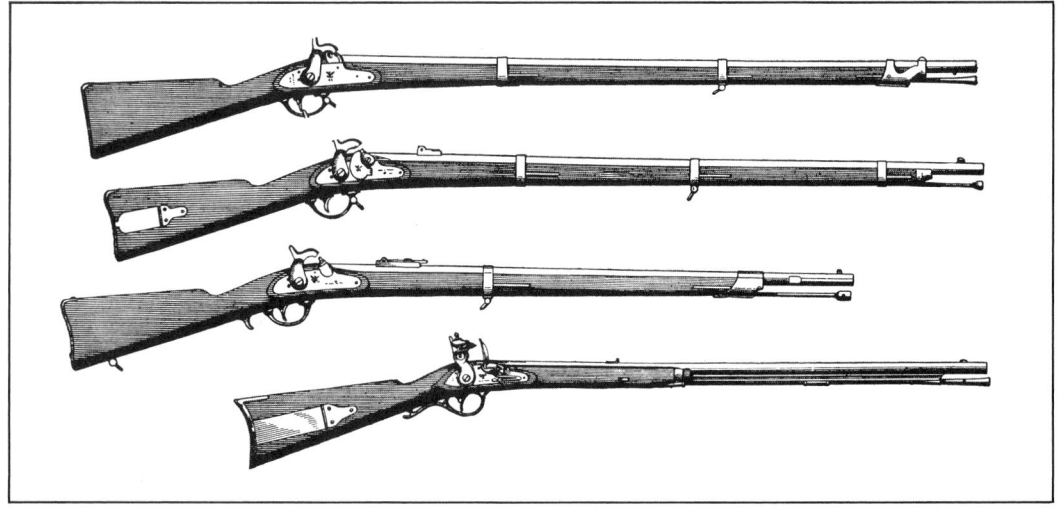

The house owned by Giles Reese was one of the few places that the rebels spared during their march. Turner's wife and three children were slaves on Reese's farm.

farm. The Giles Reese place, where Turner's wife lived, was spared, as was the farm of a childhood friend, John Clark Turner. But virtually no other homesteads were spared from an attack. It was a fearsome kind of war, swift and bloody and remorseless.

Turner split up his forces again, sending the cavalry with Hark. Upon arriving at the Porter farm with half of his army, he found that the place was empty. Everyone had fled. Turner understood immediately that word about the rebellion was out. The rebels had now lost the advantage of surprise (as he knew they would sooner or later).

Next, Turner and his men reached a strategic objective, the Barrow farm, and found the owner, a veteran of the War of 1812, hoeing in the fields. The old man fought so valiantly before he was killed that the rebels honored him by wrapping his body in a quilt and placing a plug of tobacco on his chest—this was the way that warriors were honored in parts of Africa. Barrow was the only one of their enemies that the rebels so honored. In contrast, when some of the rebels were killed later on, their bodies were mutilated shamelessly by their enemies.

By this time, Turner was riding at the back of his army, trying to coordinate the whole as his men struck from farm to farm. Billy Artis, Will, Hark Travis, and Nelson Williams had come to the forefront as natural leaders; they were Turner's lieutenants. Hark was the first among them, leading the largest detachment of cavalry.

At about 10 A.M., Turner caught up with a section of his forces at the Harris farm, only five miles from the town of Jerusalem. Their journey was half over.

As Turner rode up to them, his sword in hand, he was surprised to see how large his forces had grown. Forty insurgents, all mounted—and many of them armed with rifles or muskets—greeted him with loud hurrahs. Forty black warriors with African blood—an army of slaves riding for freedom, honoring their modern-day Spartacus (a leader of a slave rebellion in ancient Rome).

This was Turner's greatest moment, the culmination of his dreams and plans. Win or lose, he had achieved something that no other slave in America had ever accomplished: He had put together a slave army, mounted and armed and in the field, fighting for its freedom. Now they would show their owners how they could fight!

Some of the men had been drinking, though, and this worried Turner. He sternly ordered his troops away from the brandy barrels that they had rolled onto the lawn and told them to stand at attention. Then he dressed them down. He explained again that they were fighting for a cause beyond their individual freedom or pleasure, and in his magnificent preacher's voice, he commanded them to "shape up."

At this point, Turner's authority was challenged for the first time. A slave named Aaron spoke up and warned that it was time to turn back, that the rebellion did not have a chance against the white man's powerful forces.

Nonsense, Turner said. Even though the slaves were outnumbered, they could defeat the whites if enough slaves rallied to their cause.

Aaron persisted. He said that he had accompanied his master to fight in the War of 1812, and if Turner had seen as many white soldiers as Aaron had seen at Norfolk, then Turner would know better.

History has not recorded Turner's reply, much less his feelings. Certainly, he knew that there was much truth in what the fainthearted slave was saying. Half of Virginia was already up in arms and was preparing to crush the rebels. And if Virginia failed, the full strength of the United States would be brought to bear against them.

Yet Turner knew that there was no turning back. They were facing an enemy that refused to recognize their humanity, much less their right to rebel, and there was no thought of quarter or surrender. A few individuals might slip back to their slave cabins, but the leaders were known. Besides, win or lose, they had already struck a mighty blow against slavery—an army of black rebels would be an inspiration to future generations, even in defeat. Were they not free men now, if only for a day? Was it not better to die free than to live in slavery?

While Turner knew all of this, he probably knew as well that no general ever rallied his troops by preparing them for defeat. So he may have attempted to inspire his men by invoking words similar to those of David Walker's: "I think one black man is worth fifty whites. Unleash us and you have unleashed tigers." Or perhaps he drew on the history that his mother had been so careful to instill in him, reminding his men about their heritage as Africans; they were the sons of great warriors.

Harsh, scornful, soaring, bitter, poetic—whatever words Turner used, they ended the debate. The doubter was silenced, if not converted, and the general prevailed.

Yet the men who followed Turner were inspired not only by their leader's oratory but by what was in their hearts. Many of them were teenagers who would be facing a life of servitude if they gave up the fight. They knew how powerful and ruthless their enemy was, just as surely as they knew that they were fighting for a freedom that could not easily be won.

As the rebels stood in the ranks with their guns at the ready, they must have known the literal meaning of the words "freedom or death." Each man had to make a choice in his heart. He had to choose between riding with Turner, even into the jaws of death, or slipping back into a life of slavery, which was to kill them, as David Walker said, "by inches."

Almost to a man, they chose to follow Turner.

A final hurrah was shouted, and then Turner, with a gruff command, formed up his ranks. Then his army rode off, toward the next slaveowner's farm.

A map of the southeastern quarter of Virginia shows the area affected by Turner's revolt. The insurgents' march began at the Travis farm, a short distance southwest of Jerusalem.

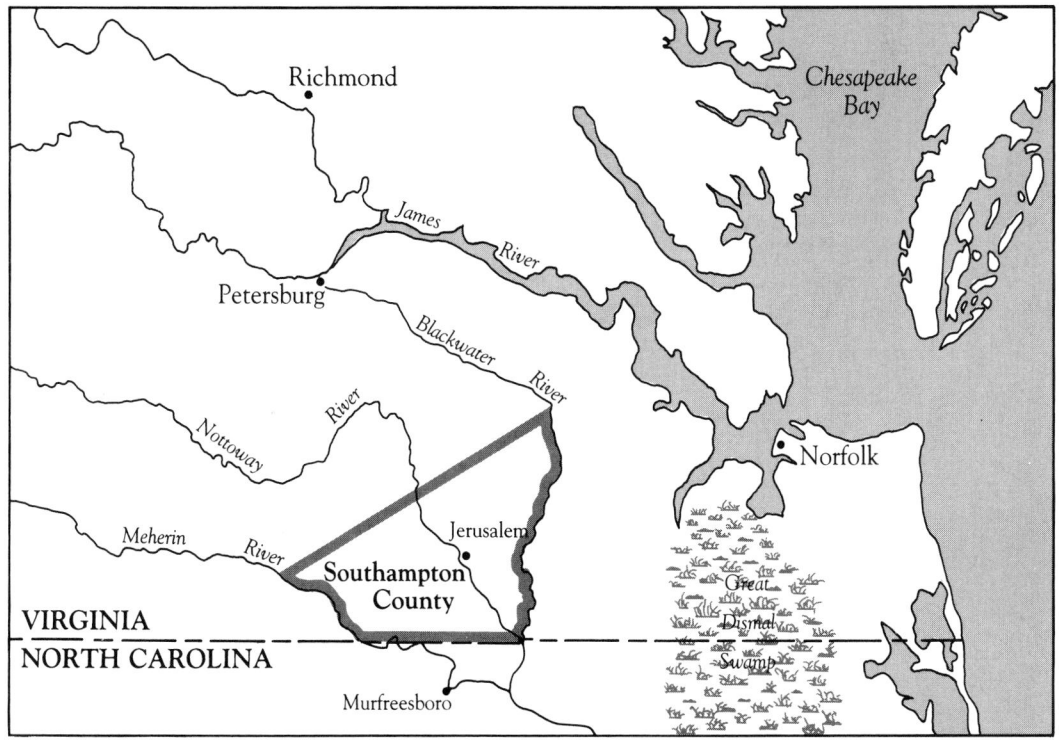

As word of Turner's rebellion spread throughout the Virginia countryside, both whites and blacks began to make speculations about where the rebel commander was intending to lead his army. Some believed that he planned to establish a base of resistance in the nearby Great Dismal Swamp.

The general continued to ride at the rear rather than the front of his troops—planning, watching, looking for signs. He knew that the going would get rougher, not easier. So far there had been little resistance. But sooner or later, the whites would stop fleeing in terror and confusion. They would rally together, and then his army would face a fight.

Until the whites started to band together, the raids continued to go smoothly. Turner adapted his tactics to fit the size of his growing army. He placed his fastest, fiercest-looking troops at the front of the column because he wanted to terrorize the whites into fleeing. The more people who saw the rebels coming, the more fear was generated.

At each homestead, the rebels charged ahead with their guns blazing and their axes flashing while shouting out their battle cries. The pattern was the same at each homestead. There was a charge, shooting, screams—and then silence.

The deeds were already done by the time Turner reached the house. The whites had been killed—men, women, and children alike. The weapons and powder had been seized. The horses had been saddled, and more men had been mounted. Then, at a sign from the general, the army would ride on toward Jerusalem.

More slave recruits joined at every farm—the strongest and boldest of the men and boys. Although it has not been recorded that any women rode with the force, they joined in the fighting at every plantation. By noon, the rebel army was 60 strong.

They began to ride openly through the fields. The element of surprise had gone with the darkness; now, speed was all. If they could gain the town of Jerusalem, they would at least be relatively secure until more slaves joined them. And then . . .

But they would let the future take care of itself. Perhaps they would flee for the Great Dismal Swamp, 20 miles to the east. Perhaps they would fight their way to the sea and hijack a ship for Haiti. Perhaps they could drive the whites from this corner of Virginia altogether. Consciously or not, Turner must have always had this last possibility in his mind, for he strictly forbade his men to burn or destroy any house or barn. His army destroyed only the people but left the livestock, houses, and barns, as though the rebels hoped that they might someday return to occupy them.

And why not? Had not they built every house, laid every fence rail, plowed and cleared every field? Whose land was it, if not theirs? ☙

7

THE
FORTUNES
OF WAR

SLAVE REBELLION! It was mid-morning on Monday, August 22, 1831, and southeastern Virginia was in a state of panic. Riders with news of the rebellion had reached Jerusalem, and the church bells were tolling the alarm. Terrified families were straggling into town across the Nottoway River, and the streets were choked with refugees. In Sussex and Greensville counties to the north and west, in North Carolina to the south, slaves were seen literally jumping for joy, kicking their heels in the air at the roadsides. It had come, as everyone in their heart of hearts had known it would someday—the long-awaited, or long-dreaded (depending on one's point of view) Judgment Day. Jubilee. Slave rebellion!

Rumors flashed through the air like summer lightning: The British had landed and were on their way; an army of 500 slaves was riding down on Jerusalem. Through it all, however, a few people learned the truth, and the truth was terrifying enough for the whites and joyous enough for the blacks. Nat Turner, Southampton County's own "Prophet Nat," was leading a slave army toward the town, leaving a zigzag trail of death and destruction behind him.

Amid all of the confusion in Jerusalem, Justice James Trezevant of the Southampton County Court scrawled a hasty note: "Terrible insurrection; several families obliterated. Send arms and men at once; a

Slowed by their consumption of too much apple brandy, the rebels delayed their attempt to seize the stores of weapons and ammunition in Jerusalem. They soon found their way blocked by large forces of white militia.

large force may be needed." The judge sent the message with a fast rider, who clattered across the boards of the Nottoway Bridge, heading north toward Petersburg and Richmond.

All of the church bells in Jerusalem were tolling in warning as lone riders, nervously looking out for armed blacks, galloped through the countryside to alert the scattered militia. Meanwhile, women and children barricaded themselves in the stores and churches, and men rolled out cider barrels, cotton bales, boards, and logs to build a hasty barricade at the bridge over the Nottoway River, all the while scanning the Murfreesboro Road for the army of 500 slaves that was rumored to be coming.

By noon, the rebel army that they feared was only three miles from Jerusalem. Behind them was a trail of death and terror, with more than 50 whites killed and the buzzards still circling. At the Waller plantation, where there had been a school, 10 children

On the day after the outbreak of the rebellion, horseback riders were carrying news about Turner's army to places as far away as Richmond, the capital of Virginia (shown here as it appeared at the end of the Civil War).

had been killed and thrown into a pile, as if in terrible revenge for all of the innocent black babies thrown from the slave ships to the sharks.

Some of the rebels, like Billy Artis, wept at the sight of the slain children. But not Turner. He viewed it all, as he was to say later, with "silent satisfaction," knowing that unrelenting terror was his only hope of scattering the whites and winning freedom for his fellow slaves. He had held his army back from attacking people whom he did not know well only once, at a cabin belonging to poor whites who held no slaves. They were people, he said, "who thought no more of themselves than they did the negroes," and therefore they were not subjected to his army's terrible retribution.

More ominous to Turner than the slaughter was the brandy. He could see that he had been too lax, and the alcohol was now taking its toll on his men in spite of his efforts to curb their drinking. Although

Jacob Williams's farm was the scene of one of the bloodiest slaughters carried out by the rebels. Some slaveowners were luckier and managed to flee from their homes shortly before the arrival of Turner's army.

Turner did not know about it at the time, one of the rebels who got drunk and fell behind was captured and then tortured and mutilated by whites.

By this time, the slaveowners had rallied, spread the alarm, and were beginning to fight back, although they were still a bit disorganized. There were two bands of militia in the field, separated and unaware of each other. One group, numbering 30 or 40 men, was led by a Jerusalem lawyer in his thirties named William C. Parker. Another group of about 20 men was led by Captain Arthur Middleton of the Southampton Militia. Both groups were following Barrow Road.

Middleton's group reached the Waller school only minutes after the slaughter there, and Middleton was so shaken by what he saw that he deserted the company and rode off to find his own family. Two other men, Alexander Peete and James Bryant, took command and rode on cautiously, looking for the slave army. It was they who found Turner's drunken soldier straggling behind in the road. They cut the tendons in his heels and left him unable to stand or walk. When another group came by, the men tied him to a tree and used him for target practice.

The retaliation of the whites—as savage as anything that Turner's army did—was already beginning.

At a little after noon on Barrow Road, Turner could see smoke from the town over the trees and hear the frantic ringing of the church bells. He formed up his men, and they started riding full speed, straight toward Jerusalem. He knew that by now there were companies of militia out looking for him. Although his men were well mounted, their weapons were poor and there was little ammunition. They had powder but only a little birdshot. So Turner showed them how gravel, poured down the barrel of a gun, would serve almost as well as lead.

Scores of slaves rushed to join the avenging army of "General Nat." Four people were killed at the house owned by Rebecca Vaughan, one of the last places attacked by Turner's band.

Turner knew that the success of his rebellion depended on gaining the town. In Jerusalem, there were arms, ammunition, and food. The whites, he knew, were panicked and terrorized to the point that they could be driven out. He hoped that once he and his men were established in the town, they could hold out long enough for larger numbers of slaves to join them, or perhaps even until the still-hoped-for intervention of the British.

It was at the Parker farm on Barrow Road, in what came to be known as the Battle of Parker's Field, that Turner faced the open fighting he had both dreaded and sought. His inexperienced and poorly armed men were to do better than he had expected.

The battlefield was not of Turner's choosing but was forced on him by the fading discipline of his soldiers. They were riding toward the town, with Turner at the rear, when they passed the Parker farm, where several of the men had relatives and friends among the slaves. Over the protests of Hark and the other leaders, the men stopped and went out back to the slave cabins to recruit more fighters—and to show off their guns and horses.

When Turner caught up with Hark, he was furious. He could hear the church bells, and he knew that the whites were gathering their forces. Angry and impatient, he left eight men by the gate to guard the front of the house and rode down the hill with Hark to the slave cabins to fetch the rest. What he saw there dismayed and sickened him: Several of his men were drunk on apple brandy, and others were bragging and showing off—when there was a war to be fought! Angrily, Turner ordered them back into formation when he heard the ominous sound of gunshots coming from the front of the house.

While Turner had gone to fetch the men from the slave quarters, the militia force of 20 men led by Peete and Bryant had come over the hill and surprised the 8 men left standing guard. Although the rebels

fought back, their ancient, single-shot guns that took a half minute to load were not much good against 20 modern military rifles. As Turner's guard fell back, the slaveowners' militia advanced on the house, thinking victory was in their grasp.

Seeing that the men around him were wavering and indecisive, Turner ordered them into battle formation and brought them around the house, into the high weeds in the field. Gaining strength from his confidence, the men followed—guns, knives, and axes at the ready.

The whites kept on advancing until Turner yelled, "Charge! Fire on them!" Yelling and screaming, the rebel army leaped into action, inspired by their leader's courage. The militia hesitated, then broke ranks and fell back in panic and disorder. These men had never seen black slaves with weapons before. Captain Bryant's horse stampeded, and he was carried away, into the woods and out of the battle.

Yelling wildly, brandishing axes and swinging gun butts, the insurgents chased the slaveowners' militia over the hill. But just then their fortunes changed.

The poorly armed rebels put up a valiant fight against the militia units, but they were finally overwhelmed at the Battle of Parker's Field and forced to fall back. The site of the battle is shown here.

Turner hoped to use the Cypress Bridge to cross the Nottoway River and then attack Jerusalem. To his disappointment, he found that the bridge was already guarded by a squad of militiamen.

One of the other groups of militia happened to be passing on the road, purely by chance, and it reinforced the fleeing whites, giving them time to reload their weapons. Regrouping while doubling in numbers, the militia counterattacked, and this time it was the rebels' turn to fall back, their guns discharged and useless.

In the withering fire of the militia's better weapons, five of Turner's best men fell wounded. Others panicked and fled into the woods. Hark's horse was shot out from under him, but Turner caught another mount on the fly and handed the reins to Hark. The two men then led a retreat into the thick forests along the Nottoway River, carrying their wounded with them. They knew what would happen to any men whom they left behind.

Stopping as soon as they were safe in the woods, Turner rallied his troops. A few stragglers joined them, bringing their force back up to 20. The men were shaken; many were bleeding. Others, the survivors said, were still hiding in the woods or fleeing across the fields.

Turner was still bound to try to take Jerusalem, which he believed was his best hope for success. By now it was clear that the main road was blocked by the militia; he had not expected so many men to arrive there so soon. But in his years of preparation, Turner had made other plans. He would cross the Nottoway at Cypress Bridge, three miles south of Jerusalem, and enter the town from behind.

Turner led his men through the brush, then down a little-known back road. But when they reached the bridge, his worst fears were realized. The little wooden span was bristling with guns and crawling with nervous, fierce-looking, armed whites. Turner's forces were too small to take it.

It was now in the late afternoon, and Turner had yet another plan. Riding fast, he and Hark led the men south, then doubled back north, across the Barrow Road again, eluding all pursuers. He was headed for the Ridley plantation—one of the largest in the county, with 145 slaves—where he hoped to recruit enough followers to make up his losses.

It was dusk by the time they reached the Ridley place, and again luck was against them. The militia had beat them there. The slaveowners had occupied and barricaded the main buildings and were keeping a close watch on the slaves.

Without letting the militia see them, Turner and Hark led their weary troops into the woods nearby, set up lookouts, and camped for the night. Their numbers were back up to 40; in spite of the guards at the Ridley place, 4 of the slaves had managed to sneak away and join them.

The men were exhausted, demoralized, and shaken by the defeat at Parker's field. More than anything, Turner knew, they needed rest. Tomorrow their fortunes might change. ◀❖▶

8

RETREATS
AND
REVERSES

———————— ❦ ————————

IT WAS MIDNIGHT. Turner had not been asleep for long when he was startled and awakened by what he later said was "a great racket." Getting up, he found some of his men mounted, some reaching for their weapons in the dark, and others scrambling about in confusion. One of the sentinels had given a warning cry, and the entire camp had fallen into disarray.

Turner suspected that it was a false alarm, yet he still sent scouts out to the edge of the woods to check up on the Ridley house. Sure enough, the militia was safely inside. They were not going to attack in the darkness.

But the damage was done; Turner's inexperienced force was already panicked. When the scouts returned, they were taken for attackers and fired on. Disorder fed on disorder, and in the ensuing confusion, many of the troops deserted.

Dawn found Turner without sleep, frustrated, low on ammunition and food, and down to 20 men again. Giving up on the idea of sleep, he ordered his men to mount. Hoping to gain recruits, they rode for the nearby Blunt plantation, where he knew there were 60 slaves.

In the gray dawn light, the place looked deserted. Turner thought that perhaps his luck was turning at last for the better: Perhaps all of the whites were with

By the morning of August 23, 1831, the rebels were in full retreat. Bands of vengeful slave-owners hunted down fugitives from Turner's army in the woods and marshes of Southampton County.

Repulsed at the Blunt plantation with heavy losses, the panicked rebels were soon scattered by white troops.

the militia at the Ridley house. Cautiously, the rebels rode through the gate, with Hark leading the way. Still cautious, Hark yelled out. There was no answer. Then he fired his gun into the air—

A thunderous volley of gunfire came from the house. It was an ambush! The horses and mules—farm animals that had been pressed into cavalry service—panicked and galloped wildly, carrying the rebels around and around the house while shotgun and rifle fire coming from behind the shutters picked them off. Hark fell, badly wounded. Horses tumbled and crushed their riders. Worst of all, some of Blunt's slaves joined in the fight on the side of their masters. Perhaps they were forced to fight; perhaps they fought willingly.

Shouting at his men to follow him, Turner retreated. This time he was forced to leave Hark and the other wounded men behind. Will helped him pull the troops back into some kind of order, and the small rebel army, exhausted and demoralized, backtracked through the woods. Many of them were wounded, most of them were without mounts, and some were without weapons.

At 10:00 A.M., they approached the Harris farm, where Turner's army had assembled and saluted their leader with bold and hopeful hurrahs only 24 hours before. However, this place, too, was crawling with whites—they were fresh troops with military rifles and horses. While Turner and his men were assessing the troops from the edge of the woods, a lookout spotted them. There was an alarm followed by shouts. Then came a blast of rifle fire, and three more of Turner's men fell dead. Among them was Will.

In response, the rebels knelt, aimed, and fired, and then turned to flee into the woods. Shouting, the militia set out after them. The skirmish in the woods was brief and bitter. The rebels, who were outnumbered, were outrun and then overwhelmed.

Turner was among the few who managed to escape, but this time he could not count on his forces to regroup. His army was in total disarray, with many dead or wounded and others scattered in every direction.

Unwilling to give up, Turner kept his sword, even though it was useless as a weapon. He found two men, then two more, and led them to a hiding place where they concealed themselves while the searching patrols almost stumbled over them. Finally, night fell around them, and, shivering and exhausted, the five men stumbled out of the woods onto a back road.

With his hand on his sword, Turner spoke softly but earnestly to inspire the men for one last try at freedom. Two of them, Curtis and Stephen, had joined the rebellion on the night before, sneaking away from the Ridley plantation, and were still fairly fresh. Turner sent them riding south, ordering them to round up as many men as they could and bring them to the woods at the Travis place, where the rebellion had begun. He would wait there for them. The revolt was not over, he insisted. They must not give up.

Accompanied by the other two men, both of them exhausted like himself, Turner struck off through the darkness. They made their way through the woods and along the back roads to the Travis place. While his two companions slept, Turner sat up all night and waited for his reinforcements to arrive.

The sun rose, but no one had come.

Turner then played his last card. He awakened his remaining two men and sent them out just as he had dispatched the others, instructing them to bring anyone whom they could find to Cabin Pond, where he had planned the revolt with his "chosen four." He would wait for them there.

They left, and he was never to see them again.

Although Turner had no way of knowing it, by this time half of his men had been killed and about

SLAVERY RECORD.

INSURRECTION IN VIRGINIA!

Extract of a letter from a gentleman to his friend in Baltimore, dated

'RICHMOND, August 23d.

An express reached the governor this morning, informing him that an insurrection had broken out in Southampton, and that, by the last accounts, there were seventy whites massacred, and the militia retreating. Another express to Petersburg says that the blacks were continuing their destruction; that three hundred militia were retreating in a body, before six or eight hundred blacks. A shower of rain coming up as the militia were making an attack, wet the powder so much that they were compelled to retreat, being armed only with shot-guns. The negroes are armed with muskets, scythes, axes, &c. &c. Our volunteers are marching to the scene of action. A troop of cavalry left at four o'clock, P. M. The artillery, with four field pieces, start in the steam boat Norfolk, at 6 o'clock, to land at Smithfield. Southampton county lies 80 miles south of us, below Petersburg.'

From the Richmond Whig, of Tuesday.

Disagreeable rumors have reached this city of an insurrection of the slaves in Southampton County, with loss of life. In order to correct exaggeration, and at the same time to induce all salutary caution, we state the following particulars:

An express from the Hon. James Trezvant states that an insurrection had broken out, that several families had been murdered, and that the negroes were embodied, requiring a considerable military force to reduce them.

The names and precise numbers of the families are not mentioned. A letter to the Post Master corroborates the intelligence. Prompt and efficient measures are being taken by the Governor, to call out a sufficient force to put down the insurrection, and place lower Virginia on its guard.

Serious danger of course there is none. The deluded wretches have rushed on assured destruction.

The Fayette Artillery and the Light Dragoons will leave here this evening for Southampton, the artillery go in a steamboat, and the troop by land.

We are indebted for the kindness of our friend Lyford for the following extract of a letter from the Editors of the Norfolk Herald, containing the particulars of a most murderous insurrection among the blacks of Southampton County,* Virginia.—*Gaz.*

NORFOLK, 24th Aug. 1831.

Turner's rebellion sent a shock-wave through America and opened many eyes to the bitter hatred that slaves felt for their oppressors. However, the Richmond gentleman whose account of the revolt was extracted in this Liberator article chose to view the revolutionaries as merely "deluded wretches."

half had been captured. Few had turned themselves in. Billy Artis had ridden from plantation to plantation, with his slave wife at his side, in a futile effort to rally support after the defeat at Blunt's. When he was at last chased down and surrounded, he defended himself with rifle fire instead of surrendering. After the shooting stopped and the whites moved in to inspect him, all they found was his hat on a stick, and his body. He had saved his last shot for himself.

Stephen and Curtis, Turner's first two messengers, had been captured less than a mile into their journey. They were taken to Cross Keys at gunpoint and locked in a log hut with other actual and suspected rebels. The little town was filled with refugees, and the whites were on a rampage. Some wanted the blacks held for trial; others wanted them beaten or executed on the spot. One female slave was tied to a tree and shot by her enraged owner.

By Tuesday, not only Southampton County but the entire state of Virginia was armed and out for blood. Judge Trezevant's message had arrived at the governor's mansion in Richmond at 3:00 A.M. on Tuesday, just as Turner was being awakened by the panic in the woods. Because the first reports indicated that the rebellion was widespread, perhaps even reaching all across the South, the governor had decided to send riders in all directions to alert and gather the militia. To play it safe, he had also ordered all units north and west of Richmond on alert. Then he had sent two Richmond units—one cavalry and one artillery—south toward Jerusalem. On top of all this, he had also dispatched a total of 2,000 guns and had ordered in the local militias of Norfolk, Portsmouth, and Petersburg.

Passions ran high all Tuesday afternoon as cavalry and artillery moved through the streets of Richmond. Rumors swept through the town, including one that a slave army was moving out of the Great Dismal Swamp and was heading toward the state capital.

Turner's revolt was quickly crushed by the white militia forces, but none of the slaveowners were prepared to rest as long as Turner remained at large. The governor of Virginia wrote this letter authorizing a reward of $500 for the capture of the rebel leader.

Mobs moved through the city, chasing and beating any blacks unfortunate enough to be seen on the street. "We experience much anxiety here," the governor said.

The seaport cities of Portsmouth and Norfolk were also seized by panic. Norfolk's mayor called in the U.S. Navy from Fort Monroe, convinced that the militia alone could not protect the city. Federal army and navy units were dispatched to Southampton County to back up the state militia.

In nearby Murfreesboro, North Carolina—just across the state line—one white man was so terrified by the news of a slave uprising that he fell dead of a heart attack on the street. All of the local militia were off at a revival meeting, and a rider was sent to alert them. He rode through the campsite, shouting, "The negroes have risen in Southampton and are

In the days immediately following the revolt, white lynch mobs carried out a wholesale slaughter of blacks in Southampton County. This crossroads was renamed Blackhead Signpost because the decapitated head of a slave was mounted on a pole by the side of the road.

killing every white person from the cradle up, and are coming this way!"

By Tuesday afternoon, the North Carolina Governor's Guards had assembled in Murfreesboro. By then, 3,000 armed whites were on the march toward Southampton County from neighboring counties in Virginia and North Carolina. This number included men from the U.S. Army and Navy, state and local militias, armed vigilante units, and lynch mobs.

The white reign of terror that soon began proved to be bloodier than the attacks by Turner and his men. Two detachments of cavalry from North Carolina killed 40 blacks in two days, decapitating 15 people and placing their heads on poles. At Cross Keys, five blacks were lynched by a mob. At a Barrow Road intersection, a man was beheaded and his skull was left to rot on a pole (called ever since "Blackhead Signpost"). Blacks were pulled from their cabins and were whipped, tortured, and lynched.

Over the next four days, more than 120 blacks were killed by lynch mobs and militia (a total that does not include the number of armed insurgents who had been captured and killed). The violence became so bad that the army commander, General Eppes, declared that any further atrocities would be dealt with under the Articles of War.

By Wednesday, August 31—10 days after the revolt had begun—49 rebels had been captured and imprisoned, including the badly wounded Hark Travis and Nelson Williams. Because slaves and free blacks were not entitled to a jury trial under Virginia law, a court trial known as "oyer and terminer" was held in Jerusalem to deal with the captured rebels. In such a hearing, the fate of each defendant is decided on by one or more judges rather than by a jury.

To give the trial an appearance of due process, lawyers were appointed for all of the slaves at a fee of $10 apiece. While the cases were being heard, the courthouse was surrounded by an angry, armed mob in the event that any of the defendants were acquitted. Every slave was priced as well as tried. Thus, when Hark was sentenced to death, the state had to pay the estate of his owner $450 for the pleasure of hanging him.

Court records and newspaper accounts show that anywhere from 15 to 20 men, and a few women, were hanged. Many more were sold back into slavery in areas with even more brutal conditions in the Caribbean and the Deep South.

The hangings went on for two weeks. Yet the panic continued in Virginia and spread west to the mountains, south into the Carolinas, and even north into Maryland and Delaware. For one question was on everyone's mind: Where was Nat Turner? ✥

9

THE FIRST
WAR

THE "GREAT BANDITTI CHIEF," as the newspapers called Turner, was still at large long after all of his fellow rebels had been captured. The slaveowners did not rest easy. Posters and descriptions of him were sent out all over the state; he was described by Jerusalem lawyer William C. Parker (the same man who had led one of the patrols to find Turner and who was later appointed to "defend" him) as "between 30 and 35 years old—five feet six or 8 inches high—weighs between 150 & 160 rather bright complexion but not a mulatto—broad-shouldered—large flat nose—large eyes—broad flat feet rather knock kneed—walk brisk and active—hair on the top of the head very thin—no beard except on the upper lip and the top of the chin . . ."

The governor of Virginia put up a reward of $500, and this was added to by others until the price on Turner's head totaled $1,100. Ironically, he was worth far more as a rebel than the $400 he had brought as a slave.

By late September, posters of Turner were up all over North Carolina as well as Virginia. Rumors multiplied among both blacks and whites: "General Nat"

For two months following the end of the rebellion, Turner managed to evade the search parties that were hunting for him. He was finally captured on October 30, 1831, by Benjamin Phipps.

was hiding out in the mountains to the west; he had escaped to the Caribbean; he had been seen in the tall reeds near the Nottoway River "armed to the teeth." One story even had him spotted on an open road, walking with a Bible toward Ohio and the West, scattering seeds of rebellion much like Johnny Appleseed planted orchards across the country.

In fact, Turner was close by, hiding out in the woods and swamps that he knew so well. He had waited two days and two nights by Cabin Pond, hoping against hope that his men would return and his army would regroup. Then he had seen white men riding around, he later said, "as if looking for someone," and he concluded that his messengers had been captured and forced to betray his whereabouts. "On this," he wrote in his *Confessions*, "I gave up all hope for the present."

Turner then broke into the still-empty Travis house, which he knew well (the upstairs bedroom floors were still dark with the blood of his late owners) and found food, candles, and blankets. Then he literally went underground, hiding himself in a shallow cave that he dug under a pile of fence rails in an open field, figuring correctly that it was the last place that his pursuers would look. He spent sometime hiding out, perhaps contacting his wife (who had been savagely beaten but had never betrayed him) but more likely staying away to protect her and the children.

For a month, Turner ventured out solely at night, seeing only the still-secret supporters who must have provided him with food and water as well as news. His heart must have been heavy. He had seen Hark and Will shot down, and he surely must have been told that they had been captured and hanged and that Billy Artis had taken his own life rather than surrender.

However, Turner never gave up hope entirely. We know this because he never gave up his sword.

Even though it was useless as a weapon, it was the symbol of his rebellion and of his command, and he kept it by his side.

This cave was Turner's home for part of the time that he was in hiding.

Turner's only hope for survival was to flee either to the West or to the sea, but individual survival had never been his goal. After all, he had escaped once and had come back for his people. So, in the end, he stayed with them, choosing to die in Southampton County rather than fleeing and living in exile.

As the days dragged on for Turner, and September turned into October, he pondered and brooded, praying for a sign that was never to come. He was almost caught on two separate occasions. One day, two slaves who were out hunting surprised him and betrayed him to their masters; he barely eluded the mob that subsequently came after him. Another time, Nathanial Francis spotted him and fired his weapon; the shot put a hole through Turner's hat. Once again he was pursued, so he dug another cave under a fallen sassafras deep in the woods. After spotting him for a second time, his pursuers knew for sure that he was in the neighborhood, and patrols with dogs began to comb the woods day and night.

On October 30, the inevitable happened. As Turner was crawling out of his carefully camouflaged tunnel, he was surprised by a white man holding a shotgun. The man, named Benjamin Phipps, ordered Turner to hand over his sword. He did, and his war against slavery was over.

Phipps tied up his captive and then fired into the air in triumph. (Ironically, Turner's captor was not a slaveowner but a poor white, of the kind whom Turner had ordered his men to spare.) Word of Turner's capture was soon out, and bells rang all across Southampton County as he was marched to a nearby plantation. Nearly a hundred people gathered around him, spitting in his face and taunting him.

Turner faced them back with a fierce pride, neither answering their taunts nor asking for mercy. A witness reported that he "just grinned" and refused to repent. At the nearby village of Cross Keys, he was beaten, then boarded up in a farmhouse for the night.

The infamous captive was carried in chains to Jerusalem on the following day. There he was taken before two judges—Trezevant and Parker—who began to question him. He answered them frankly and unrepentantly. His calm dignity amazed the reporters and observers who had crowded into the courtroom, expecting to see a crazed madman. He expressed no repentance over the deaths of the 55 to 60 whites who had been slain during the rebellion. He said only that had the rebellion been successful, "women and children would afterwards have been spared, and men too who ceased to resist."

The judges persisted. Hadn't he done wrong? they wanted to know. Didn't he feel remorse?

No, Turner insisted, he had done no wrong, even though the rebellion had failed. If he had to do it over, he said, he "must necessarily act in the same way again."

Turner's hearing was set for November 5, 1831. He was then carried to the jail, followed by an immense crowd reviling and cursing him. Inside the jail,

While Turner was in jail waiting for his trial to begin, two county judges questioned him about his revolt. The magistrates were startled to learn that Turner felt no remorse for his deeds and believed that he had been carrying out God's commandments.

THE

CONFESSIONS

OF

NAT TURNER,

LEADER OF THE LATE

Insurrection in Southampton, Va.

As fully and voluntarily made to Thos. C. Gray, in the prison where he was confined—and acknowledged by him to be such, when read before the court of Southampton, convened at Jerusalem, November 5, 1831, for his trial.

MNEMOSYNE PUBLISHING INC.
Miami, Florida
1969

Shortly before his trial, Turner had a meeting with a local lawyer named Thomas Gray, during which he discussed the reasons for his revolt. Gray later published an account of the conversation, which he called The Confessions of Nat Turner.

Barry Newsome and Thomas Haithcock, two free blacks who had ridden with him, were being held for hanging. While Turner was being chained and manacled, a white man taunted him, asking what had he done "with all the money he stole."

Turner replied coolly that he had taken exactly 75 cents. Then he turned to Newsome and Haithcock and said to them, "You know money was not my object."

Even in this grim setting, they laughed. Money? Freedom or death had been their object, and failing the one, they now were to have the other. Their motive was something that these slaveowners could not seem to understand.

On Tuesday, November 1, an elderly white man visited Turner's cell. He was Thomas Gray, a local lawyer, who had defended some of the insurgents. A friend of the jailer, he had received permission to transcribe Turner's story—his "confessions," as Gray called it—because public curiosity was "much on the stretch" to know the true story behind the rebellion.

For some reason—perhaps because Gray showed him a little decency and respect—Turner decided to talk to him. Although he told Gray the entire story, he omitted all of his rebels' names except for those whom he knew had been killed or hanged. Also, he never once mentioned his wife or his children. He explained most of his motives in religious terms, both because that was what he felt whites understood best and because he saw his devotion to freedom and liberty as a religious quest.

Indeed, when Gray asked Turner the same kind of question that the judges had asked him—Wasn't he sorry about what he had done, seeing that he was now to be punished with death?—he answered simply, "Was not Christ crucified?"

Gray ultimately attributed Turner's actions to revenge and religious fanaticism, and in several in-

NAT TURNER'S CONFESSION.

Agreeable to his own appointment, on the evening he was committed to prison, with permission of the jailer, I visited Nat on Tuesday, the first of November, when, without being questioned at all, he commenced his narrative in the following words:—

Sir,—You have asked me to give a history of the motives which induced me to undertake the late insurrection, as you call it. To do so, I must go back to the days of my infancy, and even before I was born. I was thirty-one years of age the 2d of October last, and born the property of Benj. Turner, of this county. In my childhood a circumstance occurred, which made an indelible impression on my mind, and laid the ground-work of that enthusiasm, which has terminated so fatally to many, both white and black, and for which I am about to atone on the gallows. It is here necessary to relate this circumstance —trifling as it may seem, it was the commencement of that belief which has grown with time, and even now, sir, in this dungeon, helpless and forsaken as I am, I cannot divest myself of it. Being at play with other children, when three or four years old, I was telling them something, which my mother overhearing, said it had happened before I was born—I stuck to my story, however, and related some things which went, in my opinion, to confirm it—others being called on were greatly astonished, knowing that these things had happened, caused them to say in my hearing, I surely would be a prophet, as the Lord had shewn me things that had happened before my birth. And my father and mother strengthened me in this my first impression, saying in my presence, I was intended for some great purpose, which they had always thought from certain marks on my head and breast—[a parcel of excrescences which, I believe, are not at all uncommon, particularly among negroes, as I have seen several with the same. In this case, he had either cut them off, or they had nearly disappeared.] My grandmother, who was very religious, and to whom I was much attached—my master, who belonged to the church, and other religious persons who visited the house, and whom I often saw at prayers, noticing the singularity of my manners, and I had too much sense to be raised, and if I was, I would never be of service to any one as a slave. To a mind like mine, restless, inquisitive, and observant of everything that was passing, it was easy to suppose that religion was the subject to which it would be directed, and, although this subject principally occupied my thoughts, there was nothing that I saw or heard of, to which my attention was not directed. The manner in which I learned to read and write, not only had great influence on my own mind, as I acquired it with the most perfect ease, so much so, that I have no recollection whatever of learning the alphabet, but, to the astonishment of the family, one day, when a book was shown me to keep me from crying, I began spelling the names of different objects—this was a source of wonder to all in the neighborhood, particularly the blacks—and this learning was constantly improved at all opportunities. When I got large enough to go to work, while employed, I was reflecting on many things that would present themselves to my imagination, and whenever an opportunity occurred of looking at a book, when the school-children were getting their lessons, I would find many things that the fertility of my own imagination had depicted to me before;

The Confessions *(whose first page is shown here) revealed Turner to be a man of high intelligence and moral purpose. Many people who read his statements were amazed to discover that he was not the crazed fanatic they imagined him to be.*

stances in the *Confessions*, he also put his own words in Turner's mouth. However, he seems to have recorded Turner's story pretty much as the revolt leader told it. All told, Gray was impressed by the dreaded rebel general. He said that he found Turner "for natural intelligence and quickness of apprehension, surpassed by few . . . he possesses an uncommon share of intelligence, with a mind capable of attaining anything."

Yet Gray was also horrified by what he said was Turner's "calm composure, still bearing the stains of the blood of helpless victims . . . covered with chains; yet daring to raise his manacled hands to Heaven, with a spirit soaring above the attributes of man. I looked upon him and my blood curdled in my veins." And rightly so. For what Gray was seeing was the very thing that "curdled the blood" of every slaveowner: their nightmare come to life—the slave who had seized back his own humanity with the sword.

It is not recorded that Turner had a last meeting in the jail with his wife and children. Perhaps such a meeting had already happened in secrecy, while he was still in hiding. After his capture, he seemed more careful than ever to protect them from the rage and terror that still gripped the whites of Southampton County and that had claimed so many lives of the innocent as well as of the "guilty" who had been his followers.

Turner's trial began on November 5. Such a huge crowd had gathered for it in Jerusalem that the sheriff had recruited extra deputies, fearing that the prisoner would be lynched on his way to the courthouse. The sheriff felt that it was important for Turner to be given the appearance of a fair trial.

After Turner was brought into the courtroom in chains, a clerk read the charges against him: "Nat, alias Nat Turner, a negro slave, the property of Putnam Moore, an infant, charged with conspiring to rebel and making insurrection."

William Parker, who was appointed as Turner's defense attorney, acted fairly, and on the instructions of his client (and probably to his own surprise), he entered a plea of not guilty. Turner informed his lawyer, the courtroom, and the judge very clearly that he felt no guilt whatsoever.

The first person to testify against Turner was a man named Waller who had managed to escape from one of the farms that was ravaged by the rebels. He stated that Turner did in fact command the rebels who had killed his wife and children. Turner did not dispute this.

Next, Judge Trezevant took the stand and repeated the testimony that Turner had given to him on the day after his capture. The clerk then read the long statement that Turner had given to Gray (later published as the *Confessions*), which Turner acknowledged to be "full, free and voluntary."

Turner received a quick trial at the Southampton County Courthouse. He made no effort to deny that he had committed the deeds of which he was accused, stating that only God could pass judgment on him.

That was it for the trial. Turner was quickly pronounced guilty, and he was asked by Judge Cobb, "Have you anything to say why sentence of death should not be pronounced upon you?"

"Nothing but what I've said before," Turner replied calmly.

The judge then delivered a long and passionate speech on the horrors of rebellion. His voice rose in pitch as he concluded, "The judgment of this court is that you . . . on Friday next, between the hours of 10 A.M. and 2 P.M. be hung by the neck until you are dead! dead! dead! and may the Lord have mercy upon your soul." Turner was then valued at $375, which the judge ordered to be paid to the Moore estate.

On the appointed day—November 11, 1831— Turner went unflinchingly to the death that he had chosen over slavery. He was not the first—nor would he be the last—black rebel to be hanged in the aftermath of the rebellion. In all, 50 stood trial and 21 were hanged. There were at least 20—and perhaps

Shortly after Turner's rebellion, one anguished American commented, "I foresee that this land must one day or another, become a field of blood." The sacrifices made by Turner's revolutionaries and countless numbers of other antislavery fighters helped bring on the Civil War and a new era of freedom for all black Americans.

as many as 30—more rebellion-related "legal" executions (not including outright lynchings) in neighboring Virginia counties and in North Carolina. Whether these were actually related to Turner's rebellion, or only thought to be so by the panicked whites, is not known. All told, the rebellion cost the lives of approximately 60 whites and as many as 200 blacks.

But the heavy toll of slavery and rebellion did not stop there. After all, slaves were property; and whereas hangings brought personal satisfaction to many whites, destroying property brought financial hardship. Consequently, the governor commuted the sentences of 10 convicted slaves who were then sold south. Among them were Turner's wife and daughter.

According to folklore, one of Turner's sons found his way to relative freedom in Ohio. Another is said to have stayed in Southampton County. Even today, near the town of Jerusalem (now called Courtland) there is a black storekeeper named Turner who proudly claims to be Nat Turner's direct descendant.

And well might this man be proud. For although Nat Turner's rebellion did not end in triumph, neither did it result in failure. By mobilizing and leading a slave army, he destroyed forever the notion that the slaves would not, or could not, fight for their freedom. In seeking racial justice and human rights, he became the spiritual father and political inspiration to subsequent generations of freedom fighters, from antislavery activist Harriet Tubman to the 200,000 black soldiers who took up arms against southern slaveowners during the Civil War, to such 20th-century black activists as Marcus Garvey and Malcolm X.

In black folklore, "The Second War" is a phrase that is often used to refer to the Civil War, a bloody struggle that put an end to slavery in America. "The First War" was the rebellion led by Nat Turner. ❧

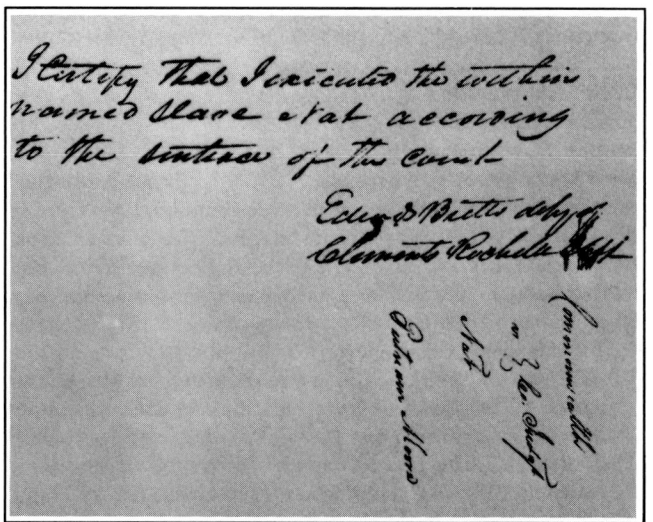

Nat Turner's Death Certificate

CHRONOLOGY

———— ❦ ————

1800	Nat Turner is born in Southampton County, Virginia
1821	Runs away from Samuel Turner's estate; marries Cherry
1822	Is sold to Thomas Moore and is forced to live apart from his family
1825	Becomes a preacher
1828	Begins to recruit men for a slave rebellion
Aug. 22, 1831	The slave rebellion begins
Oct. 30, 1831	Turner is captured
Nov. 1, 1831	Has his "confessions" recorded by Thomas Gray
Nov. 5, 1831	Is put on trial
Nov. 11, 1831	Is hanged in Jerusalem, Virginia

FURTHER READING

Aptheker, Herbert. *Afro-American History: The Modern Era.* New York: Citadel Press, 1971.

———. *Nat Turner's Slave Rebellion.* New York: Humanities Press, 1966.

Bennett, Lerone, Jr. *Before the Mayflower.* New York: Penguin, 1984.

Clarke, John Henrik, ed. *William Styron's Nat Turner: Ten Black Writers Respond.* Boston: Greenwood, 1968.

Drewry, William Sydney. *The Southampton Insurrection.* Washington, D.C.: Johnson, 1900.

Harding, Vincent. *There Is a River.* New York: Harcourt Brace Jovanovich, 1981.

Oates, Stephen B. *The Fires of Jubilee: Nat Turner's Fierce Rebellion.* New York: New American Library, 1975.

Rogers, J. A. *World's Great Men of Color.* New York: Macmillan, 1972.

Rollins, Charlemae Hill. *They Showed the Way.* New York: Thomas Y. Crowell, 1964.

Tragle, Henry Irving, ed. *The Southampton Slave Revolt of Eighteen Thirty-One.* Amherst: University of Massachusetts Press, 1971.

INDEX

PICTURE CREDITS

————— ❧ —————

TERRY BISSON is a graduate of the University of Louisville in Kentucky. He is the author of two novels, *Wyrldmaker* and *Talking Man*. He has also written articles on history and political affairs for *The Nation* and the *City Sun*. His third novel, entitled *Fire on the Mountain* and based on events in the life of John Brown, will be published by Arbor House in 1988. He lives in New York City with his wife and children.

NATHAN IRVIN HUGGINS is W.E.B. Du Bois Professor of History and Director of the W.E.B. Du Bois Institute for Afro-American Research at Harvard University. He previously taught at Columbia University. Professor Huggins is the author of numerous books, including *Black Odyssey: The Afro-American Ordeal in Slavery, The Harlem Renaissance,* and *Slave and Citizen: The Life of Frederick Douglas.*